Cold Cases:
Solved

Volume 1

18 Fascinating
True Crime Cases

Robert Keller

**Please Leave Your Review of This Book at
http://bit.ly/kellerbooks**

ISBN: 9798705110858

All rights reserved.

Table of Contents

The Darkest Shade of Evil

Lloyd Welch

The cops dubbed him Tape Recorder Man. He was six-foot tall and probably in his mid-50s. He walked with a limp. Tape Recorder Man was conservatively dressed in a brown suit, and he carried a brown leather briefcase. Inside the case was the latest model cassette recorder. On Tuesday, March 25, 1975, this individual spent hours strolling the Wheaton Plaza shopping mall in Wheaton, Maryland, a suburb of Washington D.C. He was seen demonstrating his recorder to groups of interested youngsters hanging out during their spring break. No one quite understood Tape Recorder Man's purpose in doing this. He had no product to sell, no business to promote. His only interest seemed to be in spending time in the proximity of children. In those more innocent times, no one appears to have been particularly alarmed by this. That opinion would change when two little girls went missing.

If you lived anywhere in the D.C. area during the '70s, you knew the voice of John Lyon. John was a popular host on WMAL, serving the metro area. He was also the husband of Mary and the father of Jay, Sheila, and Katherine. The family lived in Kensington, Maryland, a short half-mile from the Wheaton Plaza mall. On the morning of Tuesday, March 25, 1975, Mary Lyon gave her daughters Sheila, aged

12, and Katherine, 10, permission to walk to the mall. The girls left sometime between 11 o'clock and noon and were under strict instructions to be home by 4:00 p.m. Their mother would never see them again.

The disappearance of Sheila and Katherine would be reported to the police at 7 o'clock that evening. It would spark a massive search and dominate the news for weeks to come. As detectives began reconstructing the girls' last moments, they learned that a friend had seen them talking to an unidentified man outside the Orange Bowl restaurant at around 1:00 p.m. About an hour later, their brother Jay had seen them inside the restaurant, eating pizza together. Sometime between 2:30 and 3:00, another friend had spotted them leaving the mall, walking westward in the direction of their home. After that, they vanished.

What particularly interested the police about this timeline was the conversation with the unidentified adult male. This was the man in the brown suit, the man with the briefcase, the individual they would soon dub Tape Recorder Man. This person was immediately elevated to the top of the suspect list. Investigators were convinced that he knew something about the missing girls and might be responsible for their disappearance. A considerable amount of effort was expended to find him. In fact, the police devoted so much attention to Tape Recorder Man that they completely overlooked another suspect.

In the aftermath of their disappearance, a friend of the Lyon sisters reported to detectives that a scruffy, long-haired man had been eyeing the sisters up. In fact, he'd been so fixated on the girls that their friend, barely 12 years old herself, had decided to confront him. The man had shuffled off after she berated him for staring at Sheila and Kate. The description that the girl provided was of a white male, late teens to early 20s, shabbily dressed, scars on his left cheek, and a bad case of acne. The police attached very little importance to this report. They were fixated on their main suspect. Despite their considerable efforts, they would never find Tape Recorder Man.

The search for the Lyon sisters was protracted and intense, involving police from multiple jurisdictions, hundreds of volunteers, and even the Maryland National Guard. Vacant lots, stream beds, abandoned buildings, tracts of forest, all were combed without result. There was a reported sighting of the girls, trussed up and gagged in the back of a beige station wagon in Manassas, Virginia; there were calls from psychics and scam artists; there was a callous attempt by some sick individual to extort $10,000 from the distraught parents. And then there was a claim by a man named Lloyd Welch that he had witnessed the actual abduction.

Welch first reported his sighting to a security guard at the Wheaton Mall one week after the girls vanished. The guard then called the police and Welch was transferred to an interrogation room and asked to repeat his story. He claimed to have seen an older man, dressed in a brown suit, bundling the girls into a car and driving away with them. The man, he said, walked with a limp. Since the person he was describing was almost an exact match for their main suspect, the police were naturally interested. However, there were inconsistencies in Welch's statement, and so he was asked to take a polygraph. He agreed and failed.

That, right there, should have roused the suspicions of investigators. However, their obsession with Tape Recorder Man was still to the fore, hampering their efforts. Rather than flagging Welch as a suspect, they took him for an attention-seeker, trying to insinuate himself into the investigation, to play the hero, perhaps to cadge a reward. Welch was sent on his way with a warning not to waste police time. No one seemed to notice that he was an exact match for the man that the Lyon sisters' friend had described, the creep who had been staring so intently in their direction.

These missteps by the investigative team clearly illustrate the dangers of pre-judging a case. In any event, the investigation stumbled and stalled, faltered and ground to a halt. Two little girls had disappeared from a busy mall in broad daylight, and no one had any idea what had happened to them. Over the decades that followed, the case would haunt the Montgomery County Police Department. It was the one that everyone wanted answers to, the one that got away. Generations of detectives came and went, and many of them had a crack at it, poring over boxes of yellowing evidence, hoping to find something, anything, they might have missed. One of those was Detective Chris Homrock. In 2013, he made a breakthrough.

Homrock had been through the case file before, yet somehow had never seen one particular piece of evidence until now. It was a six-page transcript of the statement given by an 18-year-old named Lloyd Welch. Now, reading through that statement, the detective was stunned. Here was a guy who'd lied to the police, who'd failed a polygraph. Why hadn't he been looked at? It was time to redress that oversight.

Finding Lloyd Welch was easy. He was in prison in Delaware, entering the final stretch of a 33-year prison term for sexually assaulting a 10-year-old girl. The relevance of that offense was not lost on Homrock. He and Detective Dave Davis sat down with Welch on October 16, 2013. The first words out of the convicted pedophile's mouth were telling. "I know why you're here," he grinned. "You're here about those two missing girls."

From that point on, however, Welch was in full denial mode. "I didn't kill nobody. I didn't rape nobody. I didn't do nothing to those girls," he insisted. No matter what the detectives tried, they couldn't shift him from that stance. Eventually, Homrock decided on a different tactic. As he was leaving, he asked Welch what he thought had happened to the girls. Welch's answer was informative. He suggested that they had probably been raped and killed and that their bodies would then have been burned.

This would be the first of many interviews that Det. Homrock conducted with Lloyd Welch. Lloyd turned out to be a talker, who liked the sound of his own voice. He was also a compulsive liar, and not a very good one. Time and again, he talked himself into a corner, contradicting something he'd said before. Eventually, he was forced to concede that he did know something about the Lyon sisters' disappearance after all. He admitted that he had helped kidnap them but insisted that he hadn't harmed them in any way. That was done by a member of his family, he said, although the identity of this individual changed with each retelling. First it was his cousin, then an uncle, then his father.

It was time for investigators to delve deeper into the extended Welch clan. What they found was like something out of a James Dickey novel. The family had deep Appalachian roots and conformed to just about every bad hillbilly cliché ever conceived. Abject poverty, contempt for the law, impulsive violence and suspicion of outsiders, all seemed to be ingrained in the family's DNA. So too were incest and child abuse. If this band of miscreants had somehow been involved in the abduction of the Lyon sisters, then the fate of those little girls did not bear thinking about.

And Lloyd was insisting that they had been. The chief culprit, he said, was his Uncle Dick. According to him, it was Dick who'd abducted the girls, he who had drugged them and directed their gang rape and murder. Thereafter, Lloyd said, the children had been dismembered and their bodies burned.

Dick Welch was nearly 70 years old when detectives arrived to question him. That would have put him in his early 30s at the time the girls were taken. Back then he'd worked as a security guard, and he'd had a reputation for violent belligerence. Even the battle-scarred members of the Welch clan were afraid of him. Yet Dick seemed almost wounded by the idea that he'd harm a child. "As God is my witness, no," he insisted when asked. Later, he'd repeat that denial in front of a grand jury.

Lloyd's cousin Teddy Welch (one of those he'd accused as the girls' abductor, even though Teddy would have been just 11 back then) was rather more forthcoming. He described a night in 1975 when Lloyd arrived at the family homestead on Taylor's Mountain, Virginia. There he'd stoked up a fire and then hauled out two bloody duffel bags from his car, which he consigned to the flames. Two other cousins, Henry Parker and Connie Parker Akers, also recalled the incident as did some of the Welches' neighbors. They remembered the sickly stench of seared flesh that had pervaded the area for several days thereafter.

The net was closing on Lloyd Welch. Even as he continued to deny rape and murder, the evidence was continuing to stack up against him. The detectives had now learned to read between the lines of Lloyd's narrative, picking out the vivid little details that kept popping up in his stories, repeated over and over like disks in a juke box. There was the one about stalking the girls in the mall; how they were lured to a station wagon; the picture of one of the terrified children crying in the backseat of the car, while the other tried to comfort her; the grimy basement where they were kept; drugging them; the repeated rapes; the ax that had been used to kill and dismember them; a green military-style duffel bag; a bonfire. These were not passive third-party reflections. These were the recollections of someone who'd been there.

In May 2015, Det. Dave Davis went looking for the place where Sheila and Kate had been held. Lloyd had claimed that this was his Uncle Dick's basement, which was convenient since Dick's old home in Hyattsville had been torn down to make room for the new district court building. Still, Davis knew Lloyd well enough by now to know that he was probably lying. If Lloyd said that Dick Welch's basement had been the place, then almost certainly, it had not been. Far more likely was the basement of Lloyd's father's house, where Lloyd had been staying at the time.

There were new residents at 4714 Baltimore Avenue on the day that Det. Davis came calling. The tenant was happy to let him view the dingy, low-ceilinged stone vault, filled to capacity with old furniture and other junk. Entering the room, the detective instantly felt a prickling of recognition. It was almost as though he'd been here before. In a sense, he had been. He'd heard this place described before, in Lloyd Welch's rambling narratives. This dank dungeon was where two terrified little girls had been held, where they'd been repeatedly violated by multiple abusers, where their lives had been brutally snuffed out.

The following day, Davis was back, this time with a forensics team in tow. The furniture was cleared away and then the team got to work, spraying the walls and other surfaces with Luminol. This is a blood-detection agent which is triggered by the presence of hemoglobin and gives off a luminous glow when viewed under a blue light. Applied to the rear wall, it lit up the room from floor to ceiling. Someone had been killed here. No, not killed, Davis corrected himself, slaughtered.

The discovery of the murder scene finally gave the police enough evidence to charge Lloyd Welch with kidnapping, rape, and murder. This placed Welch, who had frequently voiced his fear of execution, in a precarious position. Maryland had abolished capital punishment four years earlier, but Welch would be tried in Virginia, the state which moves condemned prisoners through the legal process faster than any other.

Clearly terrified by this prospect, Welch decided to come clean. On September 12, 2017, he entered guilty pleas to two counts of felony murder in a Bedford County courtroom. The plea spared him the needle but earned him two 48-year terms. Since he is already 60 years old, he will die behind bars. Welch has since stated that he is now branded a child killer and lives in fear of a prison shank. Although others (including Lloyd's Uncle Dick and his father, Lee) are suspected of having participated in the rapes and murders, no charges have been brought due to lack of evidence.

The remains of Sheila and Katherine Lyon have never been found. Likewise, we will never know exactly what happened in that dark, dank basement. Better that we do not know. Better to remember Kate and Sheila as they were – two pretty little girls, one with long blonde hair and gold-framed glasses, the other with a stylish blonde bob – heading out for a day of fun at the mall. Better that the story ends there.

Sentence of Death

Donald Bess Jr.

Happy, outgoing, bubbly, a people person – these were the words that friends typically used to describe Angie Samota. The 20-year-old was a junior at Southern Methodist University in Dallas, Texas, studying computer science and electrical engineering. She was serious about those studies, but Angie also loved to socialize. On the night of Saturday, October 13, 1984, she invited friends Ana Kadala and Russell Buchanan to join her on a trawl of the city's most popular nightspots. Her boyfriend, Ben McCall, was also asked to join them but cried off, saying that he had an early start at his construction job. "Your loss," Angie jokingly told him as she hung up the phone.

Angie, Ana, and Russell would make quite a night of it, visiting Bennigan's and Studebaker's and ending up at the Rio Room, an exclusive members-only club. Angie, as always, was the life of the party, flitting from table to table, laughing and talking with friends. She wasn't drinking as much as her companions, though, since they'd come out in her car and she was driving. She also had plans to attend a football game early the next morning. Eventually, at around 1:00 a.m., the threesome decided to call it a night. Angie dropped Russell off at his apartment, and she and Ana then headed back to her place. Ana had planned on sleeping over, but now she changed her mind. The idea of being woken in a few hours when Angie got up to go to her football game wasn't exactly appealing. She asked Angie to drop her at her dorm room instead. After doing so, Angie stopped off at her boyfriend's apartment to say goodnight. She was there only a few minutes before heading home.

Ben McCall had barely dozed off again when he was awakened by a ringing phone. Angie was on the line and she sounded strange. "Talk to me," were the first words out of her mouth. She then started rambling on about something, sounding jittery and stressed. Ben was about to ask what was wrong when he heard a noise in the background. "There's a man here," Angie said in a whisper. "He said that he needed to use the phone and the bathroom. I shouldn't have let him in." Then, raising her voice again, she asked if there was a payphone at the convenience store near her apartment. Ben said that there was, and heard Angie relay the information to the stranger inside her apartment. Then she abruptly told Ben that she'd call him back and hung up the phone.

Ben waited less than five minutes for that call. When it didn't come, he picked up the phone and dialed Angie's number. All he got was the ringtone. Angie wasn't answering. His concerned growing, Ben pulled on a pair of jeans and a sweater. Then he ran down to his truck. His boss had recently given him a new-fangled device called a cellular phone, and he lugged this along, ringing Angie's number constantly as he raced towards her apartment. "Pick up, pick up," he urged. Those pleas went unheeded. Angie's building loomed up ahead. Ben slammed on the brakes as he entered the parking lot. Then he was out of the car and running, not even bothering to turn off the headlights. He took the stairs three-by-three to her floor, started pounding on

Angie's front door and calling her name. No response came from within.

Now Ben was in a quandary. What to do? Suddenly it struck him. Angie had asked about the payphone. Maybe her line was down. Maybe she'd gone to the convenience store to call from there. It was a vain hope and one that would go unrealized. Angie wasn't at the store and had never been there according to the clerk. Ben returned to the apartment and banged on the door again. Still getting no response, he called the police.

Officers Ken Budjenska and Janice Crowther responded to the call, arriving at around 2:40 a.m. and rousing the building manager to let them into the apartment. The officers then entered, telling Ben to stay out in the corridor. It was Budjenska who found the young woman, sprawled out nude across her bed, eyes staring blankly at the ceiling, her upper torso covered in blood, blood on the walls and the headboard, soaked into the bedding. An autopsy would reveal that Angie Samota had been stabbed 18 times, all of the wounds penetrating her lungs, eight penetrating her heart, two running so deep that they nicked her spine. She had also been raped.

Reconstructing the crime, investigators theorized that the killer had been inside the apartment when Ben McCall started banging on the door. They believed he might have been assaulting Angie at the time, probably with a knife to her throat. Perhaps Angie had tried to call out and been stabbed to keep her quiet. In any case, the police believed that the killer was someone Angie knew. Lance Johnson, an ex-boyfriend, was briefly considered but dismissed when his blood type didn't match the semen recovered from the scene. Joseph Patrick

Barlow, an SMU student who apparently had a crush on Angie and had been pestering her for a date, was cleared via alibi. Ben McCall was investigated, of course, but his blood type ruled him out.

And then there was Russell Buchanan, the young man who'd been out on the town with Angie and her friend Ana. He didn't have an alibi and he could not be eliminated by blood type since he was a non-secretor. That seemed enough to convince some investigators that he was their man. The theory was that Buchanan had showed up at Angie's apartment later that night and had talked his way in. He'd tried to convince her to have sex with him. When she refused, he took what he wanted by force and then stabbed her to death.

This theory, of course, ignored one important piece of evidence – the phone call Angie had made to her boyfriend. Ben McCall knew Buchanan, so surely Angie would have referred to him by name rather than saying that he was "a man who wanted to use the phone and the bathroom." This anomaly aside, the police placed Russell Buchanan under 24-hour surveillance, keeping it up for six months. During that time, Russell was frequently hauled in for marathon interrogation sessions where the goal was clearly to force him into a confession. Eventually, Buchanan hired a lawyer. It was only then that the cops backed off. In fact, if the Dallas police had been more attentive, they might have realized that they already had Angie Samota's killer in custody. As it was, the case went cold. It would remain so for twenty years.

In 2006, a private investigator named Sheila Wysocki called the Dallas Police Department to inquire about the unsolved homicide of Angela Samota. In fact, Wysocki's involvement with the case ran deeper than mere professional interest. She'd been a friend and roommate of Angie's at SMU back in the day. It had always irked her that a killer had walked on a case that she considered infinitely solvable.

Unfortunately, Dallas PD did not seem to share Wysocki's enthusiasm for the cold case. According to them, the rape kit had been lost during the floods of 1990, destroying any chance of a DNA match. Wysocki wasn't buying that. She kept badgering. She'd later claim that it took her "700 calls" before the police relented and assigned a detective to look into the matter. That investigator was Detective Linda Crum, and she soon discovered that the rape kit wasn't lost at all. It was securely filed away in an evidence room. From there, it was an easy matter of submitting the biological samples for testing. Those tests returned a match to a serial rapist named Donald Andrew Bess Jr., currently serving a life term in Huntsville. Bess had been convicted of three violent sexual assaults committed in Dallas in 1985. The rape and murder of Angela Samota fell right in the middle of that series.

The real tragedy is that Donald Bess should never have been given the opportunity to rape Angie Samota and snuff out her life. Bess should have been in prison, serving the 25-year term that had been handed down to him in 1978, for sexual assault and aggravated kidnapping. Even with time off for good behavior, he should have remained behind bars until at least the 1990s. Unfortunately, the laissez faire judiciary of the day had seen fit to set him free after he'd served less than a quarter of his sentence. Bess had used his freedom to embark on a renewed campaign of sexual violence against women. Angie Samota would pay a terrible price for the generosity of the parole board.

Brought to trial in June 2010, Donald Bess was found guilty of first-degree murder and sentenced to die by lethal injection. He currently awaits execution at the Polunsky Unit in Huntsville. For Angie Samota, sentence of death has already been enacted. She is buried at Llano Cemetery in Amarillo, Texas.

You're History

The police suspected murder; Peter Reyn-Bardt denied it. Malika de Fernandez, his wife of just over a year, had left him, he insisted. He didn't know where she was and, frankly, he didn't care. Their marriage had irrevocably broken down. That didn't make him a killer. He challenged them to prove otherwise.

Reyn-Bardt was right, of course. The police had nothing on him other than the slimmest of circumstantial cases. His wife had last been seen alive at their bungalow in Wilmslow, a small town eleven miles south of Manchester, England, in June 1961. Now she was missing and no one had a clue as to her whereabouts. Cheshire police thought that she might be buried in the garden and asked if they could dig it up. Reyn-Bardt told them he didn't care. They could do whatever they wanted. He had nothing to hide. That should have been a clue that Malika de Fernandez was not buried there. The police brought in a crew anyway. They found nothing.

We next encounter Peter Reyn-Bardt in the south coast city of
Portsmouth where he set up home in 1963. Over the next 12 years, he
would keep a relatively low profile. Certainly, he had no issues with
the law. Then, in 1975, he hooked up with a man named Paul
Corrigan, and the two became lovers and business partners, running a
pub. They also started cruising the streets, abducting young boys and
raping them, managing to evade detection until one of their victims, a
15-year-old, went to the police.

Arrested, tried and found guilty, Reyn-Bardt and Corrigan were each
sentenced to seven years, a ridiculously short prison term for serial
child rape. And they would not even serve their full time, walking free
in 1981 after just four years behind bars. Thereafter, Reyn-Bardt
moved to London, Corrigan to Birmingham. Less than a year later,
Paul Corrigan, along with a 16-year-old accomplice, snatched a 13-
year-old schoolboy from the streets. The child would be subjected to
hours of rape and torture before he was stabbed to death with a hunting
knife. Corrigan, arrested soon after, was sentenced to life in prison.

In 1982, Paul Corrigan informed one of his prison guards that he knew
about a murder and wanted to share the details with the police. A pair
of detectives were brought in and, to them, Corrigan told an incredible
story about his former lover, Peter Reyn-Bardt. According to Corrigan,
Reyn-Bardt had admitted to him that he'd murdered his wife.

Peter Reyn-Bardt and Malika de Fernandez were first introduced at a
party, late in 1959. The pair spent the evening talking together and hit
it off so well that, by the end of it, Reyn-Bardt had proposed. Malika
must have been stunned by this sudden declaration of intent, but she
didn't reject it outright. She asked for a couple of days and spent them

considering the proposal. Her deliberations inclined her to say yes. Granted, she barely knew the man, but what did she have to lose, really? Peter was handsome, he was charming, he had impeccable manners and grooming. He also had a great job as a high-powered executive at BOAC (the forerunner of British Airways). Within barely a day, Malika had her decision. She was going to accept. Within a week, the couple was married.

But the ink was barely dry on the marriage certificate when things began to go wrong. It started on the honeymoon when Peter was unable to consummate the union and confessed to his new bride that he was actually gay. For him, this was a marriage of convenience, a shield against the consequences of his sexual orientation. Homosexuality was still a criminal offense in Britain in 1959, punishable by jail time. Peter was also afraid that his secret might come out at work, costing him his high-paying job. His marriage to Malika was insurance against that.

One can only imagine how Malika must have reacted to these revelations. Here she was, just a day into married life, learning that she'd been duped, played, taken for a fool. She suggested an annulment, but Peter urged her to think this through sensibly. He would provide for her every need; his job with BOAC meant that she could travel whenever and wherever she wanted; he would have no objection to her taking a lover. Hell, she could have ten lovers if that was what she wanted. It was an enticing proposition, and Peter was a persuasive man. After thinking it through, Malika agreed to give it a try.

But this cozy arrangement would not go quite as smoothly as Peter had hoped. According to what he later told Corrigan, Malika had gotten greedy. Dissatisfied with the generous stipend he was providing her, she started blackmailing him, threatening to reveal his secret. On the day that she died, she had arrived at the cottage to shake him down for more money. An argument had ensued and had turned violent. Peter had put his hands on his wife's throat and throttled the life out of her. He'd then considered calling the police but had decided eventually to dispose of the body. Malika had been dismembered in the bathtub. Her body parts had been dropped into a nearby marsh.

This was an interesting story. And it became even more so when the detectives checked with their Cheshire counterparts and learned that Reyn-Bardt's wife was indeed missing and that he had long been suspected of killing her. With Paul Corrigan's statement in hand, detectives of the Cheshire Constabulary tracked down Reyn-Bardt to the upscale London suburb of Knightsbridge and arrived to question him. Reyn-Bardt agreed to talk but, as always, denied everything. The cops left empty-handed. They would likely have remained so but for a chance discovery the following year.

On May 13, 1983, a team of commercial peat cutters was working a bog at Lindow Moss, just outside of Wilmslow. Andy Mould and Stephen Dooley were operating the conveyor when they noticed something unusual, a round, football-sized shape. Closer inspection revealed that it was a skull, with remnants of hair, soft tissue, and brain matter still intact. The men stopped the belt and called their supervisor. He called the police.

Twenty years had passed since the disappearance of Malika de Fernandez. Yet no one was in any doubt as to who the head belonged to. The missing woman had been found at last. This time, there would be no way for Reyn-Bardt to talk himself out of trouble. This time, there was hard evidence.

Peter Reyn-Bardt hadn't expected another visit from the police so soon. He was readying himself for another session of denials when a detective showed him a picture of the skull they'd found and revealed its location. Then Reyn-Bardt's shoulders visibly sagged and he let out a sigh. "It's been so long that I thought I would never be found out," he said. Later, he'd make a full confession, telling much the same story that Corrigan had related to the police. His wife was blackmailing him; he could no longer keep up with her financial demands; he feared arrest and losing his job; the two of them had argued; he'd been unable to stop himself once he started squeezing her throat. He had never intended murder, he said, but once Malika was dead, he'd had no option but to dispose of her. The alternative would have been a short walk to the gallows. The body, as they already knew, had been dismembered and consigned to the murky depths of the bog.

Peter Reyn-Bardt's trial was scheduled for Chester Crown Court in December 1983. In the meantime, the prosecution was preparing its case, a process that included sending the head to Oxford University for further analysis. The results of those tests would leave everyone involved with the case stunned. Carbon dating estimated the age of the skull at nearly 1,800 years. This wasn't Malika de Fernandez, this was a woman who had died around 250 AD, during the Roman occupation of Britain. The thick mud on the floor of the marsh had encased the skull and preserved it. Peter Reyn-Bardt had confessed under an entirely false premise.

It was about as delicious a case of poetic justice as anyone could dream up. Hearing that the head was not that of his murdered wife, Reyn-Bardt filed a motion to withdraw his confession but was denied. He was ultimately convicted of murder and sentenced to life in prison. He died at Norfolk and Norwich Hospital on August 17, 1995, while still incarcerated. Two more bodies have since been pulled from the bog at Lindow Moss, both dating to Roman times. As for Malika de Fernandez, she remains among the missing.

Cold-Blooded

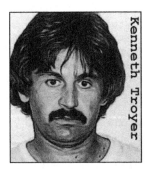

Occupying just 40 blocks in the South Bay region of Greater Los Angeles, Hermosa Beach, California, is a great place to live. Hermosa means "beautiful" in Spanish, and this little community certainly lives up to that description. With all-round great weather, beautiful beaches, a thriving cultural scene, and fantastic restaurants, it is easy to see why anyone would want to call this place home. Quite aside from that, there's the crime rate, exceptionally low for Southern California, and virtually zero when it comes to violent crime. Hermosa records only a couple of murders a decade, so when one does occur, it is big news. And when the victim happens to be the ex-wife of a celebrity, it dominates the front pages.

You've probably never heard of Karen Klaas, but you've almost certainly heard of her former husband. Bill Medley was one half of The Righteous Brothers. You can hear his distinctive bass-baritone voice on such hits as *You've Lost That Loving Feeling*, *Unchained Melody*, and *(I've Had) The Time of My Life*, a duet he recorded with Jennifer Warnes. Bill Medley received a Grammy for that performance, and he has also been inducted into the Rock 'n Roll Hall of Fame. The singer married Karen O'Grady at the very start of his music career in 1964. The couple would have a son together, but the marriage didn't last, and they divorced in 1970. Despite this, they remained on good terms. Karen later remarried, tying the knot with Gerald Klaas in 1972.

January 30, 1976, was not the kind of day that you normally associate with Southern California, even in the midst of winter. It was cold, blustery and overcast, with periodic squalls of rain. Karen Klaas had dropped her 4-year-old son at his pre-school that morning and then returned to her house. She had a coffee date with friends later, but this was a date that Karen would not keep. While she'd been out, an intruder had invaded her home. He was hiding in a bedroom when she entered and crept up behind her, brandishing a knife he'd taken from the kitchen. This he used to subdue the 32-year-old mother of two, to force her into submitting to his demands.

Karen was subjected to a savage rape, right there on her marital bed. Then, after her assailant had satisfied his carnal needs, he picked up Karen's pantyhose from the floor and wrapped them around her throat. Pressure was applied, cutting off the unfortunate woman's air supply. The assailant maintained his grip, staring pitilessly into his victim's face even as her beautiful features were distorted into a grotesque death mask, as her eyes bulged and her skin turned an unearthly hue, as her struggles subsided and she went limp. Then he got up from the bed, rearranged his clothes, and walked casually from the house, leaving through the front door, bustling past Karen's worried friends as they arrived to check on her.

Those friends had become concerned when Karen hadn't shown up for their coffee date, which was quite unlike her. Now, they arrived to find her ravaged body. Miraculously, Karen was still alive, although only barely. She was rushed to the hospital, where she would remain, comatose, for five days. She breathed her last on February 4, 1976. This was now a murder inquiry.

As Karen's distraught family, including former husband Bill, prepared to lay her to rest, the police got to work tracking down her killer. They had a description of the man, of course. Karen's friends had seen him leaving the house. They'd described the suspect as "shaggy-haired and bearded, dressed in a trench coat and blue jeans." The police had also retrieved biological material from the crime scene. In a modern context, this would have been significant. Back then, it was of limited use. Still, the evidence was bagged and securely stored, ready to be matched against a suspect if and when one was apprehended. It would remain there for the next 40 years, as the murder of Karen Klaas went unsolved.

To someone living in the 1970s, the technologies that we take for granted today would have seemed like science fiction. Sure, we don't have the flying cars and robot servants promised in the Jetsons, but we do have the internet and smart phones and photo-realistic video games; we do have electric vehicles and gene editing and space-based telescopes. To a police officer working back then, the idea of identifying a criminal by his genetic material would have seemed like a wish too good to be granted. Yet modern policing does have such a tool, and DNA fingerprinting has fast become the very cornerstone of detective work. It has also become the primary method for re-evaluating old cases. In 2016, the approach was applied to evidence from the Klaas case.

Actually, investigators had revisited the case before, back in 1999 and again in 2011. Then, submissions to state and federal databases had failed to find a match. Now, the police were ready to try a new (and somewhat controversial) approach – testing for familial DNA. This method aims to find a near match to the crime scene evidence, a match that would indicate a familial link to the unnamed suspect. This then allows law enforcement to narrow its search and to test any potential suspects that it identifies. In this instance, the query returned a match, flagging a sibling of the man that investigators were seeking. Soon they had a name. Kenneth Eugene Troyer was a career criminal with a rap sheet that ran to several pages. The only problem was, Troyer was dead. He'd been shot and killed by police back in 1982.

Kenneth Troyer had been serving a prison term for second-degree burglary at the time. On January 30, 1982, he'd pulled off an audacious escape from the California Men's Colony State Prison in San Luis Obispo. He then traveled to Orange County, where he launched a one-man crime wave, committing 19 burglaries, three armed robberies and several sexual assaults during the six weeks that he was at large. In fact, the authorities considered Troyer so dangerous that they formed a task force dedicated to his recapture. Eventually run to ground, Troyer refused to surrender and opened fire on law officers. He was killed in the resultant gun battle.

Any doubt that Kenneth Troyer was the killer of Karen Klaas was removed when biological material from the original crime scene was matched to a sample obtained from the coroner's office. The police also learned that Troyer had been living with his brother, just a few blocks from the Klaas residence, at the time of the murder. Given Troyer's M.O., it is likely that he'd broken into the house with the intention of burglarizing it. It was to Karen's terrible misfortune that he was still inside when she returned home. Had she gone to meet her friends directly, she would likely have lived.

And so the murder of Karen Klaas was solved, ending 40 years of anguished speculation for her family. The Klaas murder was only the second to be resolved using familial DNA, and the method remains controversial, banned in many states because of civil liberties concerns. These objections are merited, of course; our personal freedoms must and should be vigorously defended.

But perhaps opponents of the technology should consider the first criminal to be caught via a familial DNA test. Lonnie David Franklin Jr., a.k.a. the "Grim Sleeper," was a serial killer responsible for the deaths of at least 25 women. He was captured in 2010, ultimately convicted, and sentenced to death. Franklin would not keep his date with the executioner. He died in prison on March 28, 2020. Without familial DNA, though, Lonnie Franklin would have had an additional ten years out on the streets. Lives would have been lost.

Deliver Us from Evil

It was 9:15 on a Sunday evening in October 1989, far too late for a couple of eleven-year-olds and a ten-year-old to be out on the streets. Still, this was a safe neighborhood, and Jacob Wetterling had permission. Jacob and his younger brother, Trevor, were home alone that night while their parents attended a dinner party. They had a friend, Aaron Larson, staying over, but the three of them soon became bored. That was when Jacob phoned his mother to ask if they could go to the local Tom Thumb store to rent a video. Patty Wetterling responded with an emphatic "no." She didn't want them riding their bikes in the dark.

But the boys didn't leave it at that. Instead, they employed a tactic that every parent will be familiar with. Jacob's next call was to his dad. Jerry Wetterling listened patiently as his son explained the plan. He and Trevor would tape flashlights to their handlebars, Jacob said, and they'd wear reflective vests. The store was just four blocks away and they'd ride directly there and come straight home. Aaron would be with them, and they'd stick together. In a small town like St. Joseph, Minnesota, what was the worst that could happen? Chuckling at his son's persistence, Jerry eventually agreed. Jacob let out a whoop of delight when permission was granted.

Jacob was good to his word. He and his brother did not linger at the store. They checked out their video and then started back on the short ride home. But they'd covered only about half the distance when a man suddenly stepped from the darkness and blocked their path. The man was dressed entirely in black and wearing a stocking mask. He was also holding a gun which he now used to threaten the boys. He ordered them to push their bikes into a ditch and to lie face down on the ground. Then he started questioning them, asking their ages. When Trevor said that he was 10, the man ordered him to his feet and told him to run into the woods. "Don't look back or I'll blow your head off," he warned. Trevor had no doubt that he'd carry through on the threat.

Next, the man ordered Jacob and Aaron to stand. Then, after running his gaze over the boys' faces, he told Aaron to run, repeating the threat he'd issued earlier. Aaron did as he was told and made a dash for the tree line. There he found Trevor, crouching in the dark. The last they saw of Jacob, he was being dragged away by the man in the mask. Then they heard a car start up. That was when Trevor broke cover and sprinted for home, Aaron in his wake. Just minutes later, Trevor was on the phone, breathlessly telling his dad what had happened.

A search was launched that night, a considerable effort that involved every officer in the St. Joseph police department and endured for several days. It came up empty. Since this was a kidnapping, the FBI was also alerted and sent agents to assist. But even the considerable resources of the Bureau could not locate Jacob nor find his abductor.

Days passed, then weeks, then months without success. Jacob Wetterling seemed to have vanished into thin air.

St. Joseph, Minnesota was a safe place to live back in the '80s. It still is. But predators lurk in even the most secure of locales, and this little slice of Midwest America was no exception. The abduction of Jacob Wetterling was not the only assault on a juvenile around that time. Between the summer of 1986 and the spring of 1987, at least five teenage boys were attacked and sexually molested in nearby Paynesville. More recently, in January 1989, a 12-year-old named Jared Scheierl had been kidnapped, sexually assaulted and physically threatened by an adult male. That crime had happened in Cold Spring, Minnesota, just 12 miles from St. Joseph.

What was of particular interest to the police was that the perpetrator of the Scheierl assault had been armed with a gun and had threatened to "blow the victim's head off." These were the exact threats that had been made against Trevor Wetterling and Aaron Larson. The description given by Jared Scheierl also matched the one that Trevor and Aaron had provided. The perpetrator was Caucasian, around 5'8" and between 40 and 50 years old. He was powerfully built with broad shoulders. He spoke in a low, raspy voice.

This description would lead investigators to several suspects, including a man named Danny James Heinrich who had already been investigated multiple times for sexual assaults on children. Heinrich was questioned but ultimately released when the witnesses failed to identify him from a photo array After that, the leads quickly dried up and the case went cold. It would be revived, decades later, by a most unlikely pair of investigators.

In June 2010, federal agents swooped down on a farm near the Wetterling abduction site and handed a search warrant to the owner. An anonymous tipster had suggested that Jacob Wetterling might be buried on the property, and so forensic experts spent days sifting through the dirt for clues. Truckloads of earth were then driven away from the site for testing at a lab. The FBI also announced that it had identified a "person of interest" and brought this individual in for questioning. However, the man was later released without charge. The case had stalled again.

And it would likely have remained so but for the efforts of a blogger named Joy Baker. Baker had been 22 years of age when Jacob Wetterling was taken. She could still remember the news bulletins, the 'missing' posters, the heartrending pleas of Jacob's mother for her son to be returned to her unharmed. Now, with the FBI renewing its interest in the case, her own curiosity was piqued. She was as disappointed as anyone when the latest investigative effort came to nothing.

But Joy wasn't about to sit around and let the case fade back into oblivion. She started her own inquiry, visiting the video store, the abduction site, following the route that the boys had taken on that fateful night. Soon she had recruited another to her cause, Jared Scheierl, who had been abducted and sexually molested as a 12-year-old, possibly by the same man. Together, these amateur sleuths began tracking down other child victims in the area. What they uncovered convinced them that Jacob Wetterling had likely been taken, and likely killed, by a serial rapist with a taste for young boys.

In fact, Baker was so convinced of this that she passed on her findings to the Stearns County Sheriff's office, hoping that the case would be reopened. Unfortunately, the cops were skeptical of her conclusions. Many of the cases that were highlighted had never been reported. Even if the accusations were true, the M.O. in these attacks was different. The boys had been released after they were assaulted. They had come home. Jacob Wetterling had not.

Disappointed by the response of law enforcement, but not discouraged, Baker and Scheierl kept up the pressure, both directly with the Sheriff's office and through the media. Suddenly, the Wetterling case was getting airtime again. Questions were being asked. It was a segment on John Walsh's CNN TV show "The Hunt" that eventually tipped the balance. After that segment aired, the FBI announced that it was reopening the investigation.

In 2015, DNA evidence from Jared Scheierl's 1989 sexual assault was retested. It returned a match, to well-known pedophile and one-time Wetterling suspect, Danny James Heinrich. Unfortunately, the statute of limitations had run out on this particular crime. Heinrich couldn't be charged even if he admitted assaulting Jared. However, with clear similarities to the Wetterling abduction, there was probable cause for a search warrant. That search would turn up nothing to link Heinrich to Jacob Wetterling's disappearance. It would, however, land Danny Heinrich in serious trouble. When the Feds checked his computer, they found a large cache of child pornography.

Danny Heinrich, St. Joseph's own personal boogeyman, was staring down the barrel. The child porn charge was going to land him a long jail term. If the police were then able to uncover links to other crimes, particularly to the disappearance of Jacob Wettering, he was looking at spending the rest of his days behind bars. Heinrich was therefore more than willing to listen when a deal was suggested. He would plead to federal child pornography charges and accept the maximum sentence – 20 years. All other charges would be dropped. The condition was that Heinrich had to tell what he knew about Jacob Wettering's disappearance and reveal the location of his body. Backed into a corner, with little room to maneuver, Heinrich agreed.

Now, finally, the truth about Jacob's disappearance would be known. Jerry and Patty Wettering would have closure, even if it was not what they wanted to hear. According to Heinrich, he had dragged Jacob away from the abduction site to his car. He'd bundled the boy inside and handcuffed him. He'd then driven Jacob to a gravel pit near Paynesville, where he had sexually molested him, then strangled him and buried his body. A year later, he'd returned to the site and found the corpse partially uncovered. He'd then moved the remains to a different location. Heinrich also added one other detail, one that seemed to amuse him. The gun that he'd used to intimidate his victims had never been loaded, he said.

On September 1, 2016, Heinrich led investigators to a pasture near Paynesville, about 30 miles from the abduction site. Here, human remains were unearthed. Jacob Wetterling's bones were still draped in the clothes he'd been wearing on his last, terrifying night on earth. He would be identified by dental records two days later. "Jacob has been found and our hearts are broken," his mom, Patty, told the media.

Danny Heinrich, of course, would not be tried for Jacob's murder. He had his deal with the authorities – 20 years at a federal prison in

Devens, Massachusetts. With good behavior, he might expect to be out in 17. But perhaps Heinrich should have paid closer attention to the conditions of his plea agreement. The state of Minnesota is still entitled to bring civil charges against him after his federal term ends, keeping him behind bars as a sexual predator. Given the danger he poses, it is very likely that the authorities will exercise that option. As Judge John Tunheim said at his sentencing, "This crime is so heinous, so brutal and awful, that it is unlikely society will ever let you go free."

The Janitor

Many of us remember a guy like this from our school days: the creepy janitor who pays unwanted attention to pretty girls, the creep who always seems to be working near the sports fields when there is a cheerleading practice, the guy the kids spread nasty rumors about, calling him a sicko, a pedophile, or even a serial killer. At Shawnee Mission East High School, in the small Kansas town of Prairie Village, that guy was John Henry Horton.

Now, it would be fair to say that not everyone held this viewpoint. John Henry Horton was a man who split opinions. Some said that he was a blowhard and a braggart. Others called him a caring, family man, dedicated to his job and to the local chapter of the American Legion. His wife, Sharon, was clearly devoted to him, and his supervisor at the school appreciated his hard work. John Henry was never one to complain about long hours or about picking up an extra shift. He was doing just that on the afternoon of Sunday, July 7, 1974.

Also at the school that day or, at least, passing through it, was a 13-year-old named Lizabeth Wilson. Liz was a keen swimmer who often visited the public pool, just a short, three-block hike from her home. Usually, that walk involved a shortcut across the high school parking lot, and this was the route that Liz and her 11-year-old brother, John, followed this day. They would remain at the swimming pool until around 7:15 p.m. when they started for home, with John running ahead and Liz calling to him to slow down. John, as is the way with kid brothers, ignored these pleas. In fact, he ran even faster, rounding the school building and then sprinting up the incline on its south side. A quick glance over his shoulder told him that Liz was still following, and so he kept going, stopping only when he reached the top of the hill. Now, winded, hands on knees, he looked back along the trail. His sister was nowhere to be seen.

John waited a few moments longer. Then he called out his sister's name. Getting no response, he jogged to the front of the school building and peered around it, fully expecting to find Liz there, hiding from him. When he didn't see her, he ran to the other side of the school. Liz wasn't there either. Oh well, John decided, if his sister wanted to play games, she'd have to play them alone. He wasn't hanging around. John started jogging back up the hill. He was home, watching TV, when his parents arrived 30 minutes later.

Liz's parents were somewhat annoyed that their daughter wasn't home. She knew better than to be out at this hour. Her mom immediately got on the phone, calling Liz's friends, trying to locate her, becoming increasingly concerned with each passing moment. When it became clear that Liz was not at a friend's house, her frantic parents rounded up their neighbors and launched a search for her, back along the route to the swimming pool. That search included the high school campus, but it turned up no trace of the missing girl. Within a couple of hours, the Wilsons had called in the police.

Since Liz had gone missing in the vicinity of Shawnee Mission East High, much of the police activity was focused here. On July 8, the day after Liz's disappearance, detectives requested time cards from school administrators, in order to determine who might have been in the building at the time. One of these immediately attracted attention. John Henry Horton had not only been working that afternoon, but he'd taken a three-hour dinner break. Since this had started just after 8:05, within an hour of Liz's disappearance, it seemed suspicious. The janitor had some questions to answer.

Sharon Horton seemed surprised when a pair of detectives showed up at her home that morning. She told the officers that her husband was at an unemployment office and directed them there. Horton was cordial enough when the officers approached him. He listened attentively when they explained why they were there but said that he knew nothing that would help with their inquiries. The cops then asked if they could search his vehicle, and Horton said yes. What the officers found inside immediately elevated him to the top of the suspect list.

First, there were three bottles of chloroform, a can of ether, a gallon bottle of sulfuric acid. Then there was a butcher knife, a length of cord, and two canvas trash bags. In the passenger compartment, the officers found two throw rugs, a pillow, and a long strand of hair. Horton had answers for most of these items. He admitted stealing the knife, the acid and the chloroform from his employer. The butcher knife, he planned on giving to his wife, he said; the acid was for an experiment and the chloroform was to get high. The officers then asked if they could bag the items as evidence, and Horton said they could. He also agreed to hand over the clothes he'd been wearing the previous day, and these would raise further suspicion. Horton's underpants had a fleck of blood on them. He claimed that it must have gotten there while he was having sex with his wife, who was menstruating at the time. Sharon would later back him up in this assertion.

But this was not the only blood evidence that the detectives found on Horton. The officers had observed fresh scratches on his forehead and behind his right ear. Later, at the Prairie Village police station, they would ask him to remove his shirt, and they now saw that he had further scratches on his back, forearm, and thigh. But, as always, Horton had a slick answer to explain these away. He claimed that he'd scratched himself while working on his car.

In fact, Horton used this same excuse to justify his three-hour absence from the school. According to him, he'd left the campus to get something to eat but had run into car trouble along the way. He'd therefore pulled the vehicle into a grocery store parking lot and had spent the next two hours trying to fix the problem. He'd returned to the school after 10:00 p.m. and had continued working on the car there. The repair had necessitated him crawling under the vehicle, and that was how he'd scratched himself. Eventually, he'd been able to get the car running smoothly, and he'd then clocked out and driven home.

To the officers who questioned him, every word out of John Henry Horton's mouth sounded like a lie. They were convinced that he knew more than he was saying about Liz Wilson's disappearance. And their conviction was only strengthened when they talked to a group of cheerleaders who'd been practicing on the school lawn that Sunday afternoon. According to the girls, Horton had interrupted their session to ask if any of them needed to come into the school building. He'd then homed in on one girl in particular and asked if she wanted to come inside for the band concert. There was no band concert scheduled that day.

Two days later, two Shawnee Mission students came forward to recount their own strange encounter with John Henry Horton on that Sunday afternoon. The girls said that they had been playing tennis at the public courts, close to the school. They were on their way home, passing the school building, when the janitor approached. He said that he needed their help to shut off a water valve that was too high for him to reach and asked if one of them would accompany him and stand on his shoulders to turn off the water. The girls said no. Later, when officers checked on the valve in question, they found that it was just 18 inches off the ground.

So Horton had tried to lure at least two other girls on the day that Liz Wilson went missing; he had blood on his shorts and scratches on his back; he had chloroform and a butcher knife in his car; he had three missing hours that were inadequately accounted for. It should have been enough to arrest him on suspicion of murder. Except that it wasn't. Liz Wilson had still not been found, and there was no physical evidence linking Horton to her disappearance. There was little point in putting him on trial only for him to be acquitted and to gain double indemnity protection in the process.

In January 1975, a construction team was breaking ground at the site of the new JC Penney Distribution Center in Lenexa, Kansas, when they found a human skull. They immediately called the police, and work was stopped while the site was searched, surrendering several more human bones. The site had previously been an alfalfa pasture, and the farmer who'd owned it recalled that he'd smelled something unpleasant when harvesting the field in July the previous year. He'd assumed it was a dead animal and hadn't investigated further.

Now, though, the bones were brought to the county coroner who concluded that they were all from the same person, a Caucasian female in her late pre-teens/early teens. The technology of that time did not allow for a more conclusive identification. Liz Wilson's parents, though, were in no doubt. They believed that their daughter had been found. Later, the remains would be brought to Iowa and buried in a family plot. They were exhumed in 2003 for DNA testing and, at that time, it was confirmed. The bones were all that remained of 13-year-old Lizabeth Wilson.

And where had the child's suspected killer been in the intervening 29 years? Horton had left Prairie Village soon after Liz's disappearance. In the early '90s, he'd shown up in the tiny, north-central Missouri burg of Callao, population 300. There, he had become a town councilman as well as the volunteer fire chief. However, his old demons eventually resurfaced, and he was arrested for peeping through windows at teenage girls. A guilty plea to first-degree trespassing saw him slapped with a $500 fine, but he was now persona non grata in Callao. In 1995, he and Sharon moved to a mobile home outside of Canton, Ohio. He was still living there in 2001 when events in Prairie Village started to turn against him. The local police, working in conjunction with the Kansas Bureau of Investigation, had decided to reopen the Wilson case.

The technology that had prompted this move was, of course, DNA profiling. The police still had the hair that they had retrieved from Horton's vehicle at the time of the original inquiry. Now they submitted this to the FBI lab, to be compared against hairs obtained from a hairbrush supplied by the Wilson family. The results were not quite as conclusive as the investigators had hoped. All that the FBI would confirm was that the hairs were "microscopically similar." Nonetheless, the Johnson County D.A. decided to go ahead with a prosecution. It was now or never. Horton was arrested at his home, trying to escape through a rear window while Sharon delayed the officers at the front door.

In truth, the prosecution case was not much stronger than it had been back in 1975. However, there was one piece of evidence that tipped the balance towards conviction. The D.A. now had a theory as to how the murder had been committed, and he had a witness to back it up. Joy Creager had been a 14-year-old, living across the street from the Horton family in 1974. That summer, Horton's niece, Cindy, had come to stay, and she and Joy had become friends. One night, Horton had asked the girls if they wanted to get high. They'd agreed and Horton had driven them to a local golf club. There, sitting under the stars on the green, Horton had produced a bottle of chloroform. He'd poured some of the liquid into a rag and convinced Joy to take a sniff. Joy had passed out almost immediately. When she regained consciousness some time later, her jeans were pulled down and Horton had his fingers inside her vagina. She'd been so embarrassed by the incident that she'd told no one about it at the time.

This, the prosecution argued, was Horton's familiar M.O. He'd lure a girl to a quiet location, knock her out with chloroform and then molest her while she was unconscious. However, with Liz, he'd used too much and had been unable to revive her. That left him with a body to dispose of, and he'd done so by sneaking it out to his car and transporting it to the alfalfa field near Lenexa, where Liz's remains would later be found. Although this may sound like an accidental death, Horton had taken Liz's life while committing another crime, and that made it murder.

John Henry Horton was found guilty of first-degree murder in January 2005 and sentenced to 15 years to life. That conviction would later be overturned, but the second trial ended the same way – guilty. This time, the appeal was turned down by the Supreme Court, meaning that Horton will remain behind bars for the foreseeable future. He was turned down for parole in 2018. The killer custodian had escaped justice for nearly four decades. It is time for him to pay the price for his crimes.

Last Night

Clarence Dixon

Deana Bowdoin was getting ready to take on the world. The 21-year-old Arizona State University student was bright, pretty, and popular, with a work ethic that had seen her rise to the upper echelons of her class. There was every expectation that she'd graduate with honors. Deana was also close to her parents, so when they invited her to attend a family dinner on the night of January 6, 1978, she gladly accepted. The group sat down to a pleasant meal at a restaurant in Tempe, Arizona. When the party eventually broke up at around 9:00 p.m., Deana said her goodbyes and headed for the Monastery Bar, where she'd arranged to meet a female friend. The pair would remain at the bar until 12:30 a.m., when they exchanged hugs in the parking lot and went their separate ways. They promised to "do this again soon." That was a promise they'd never keep.

A short while later, Deana's boyfriend arrived at her Tempe apartment in the company of his brother. However, Deana's car was not in the parking lot and so the boyfriend left, drove his brother home and returned later, at around 2:00 a.m. This time, Deana's car was parked in its usual slot, and so the young man headed upstairs, used his key in

the lock and entered the apartment. He could never have expected the
nightmare that awaited him within.

Deana lay unmoving on her bed, a macramé belt pulled tightly around
her neck, her face contorted into a horrific death mask. Her clothing
was disarranged and she was bleeding from several injuries to her
chest which may have been knife wounds. A dark patch of urine
stained the bedclothes and the room reeked of it. Rushing forward, the
young man worked with unsteady hands to loosen the belt. Then he
ran for the phone and dialed 911. When the first responders arrived, he
was applying CPR to his girlfriend, desperately trying to resuscitate
her.

But there was no reviving Deana. The young woman had been
savagely attacked, strangled with the belt, knifed three times in the
chest. An autopsy would determine that she had also been raped.
Semen would be recovered from her vagina and from her underwear.
Who might have committed this terrible crime? The police had only
two suspects, Deana's boyfriend and his brother. Both men willingly
submitted biological samples for comparison and were cleared by that
method. With nothing else to go on – no witnesses, no fingerprints, no
other forensics – the investigation soon ran into trouble. It would end
up, eventually, as a cold case, one that the police held out very little
hope of solving.

What investigators didn't know at the time was that the man they
sought, the man responsible for this atrocity, was hiding in plain sight.
His name was Clarence Wayne Dixon, and he lived just 500 feet away
from Deana Bowdoin's front door. Dixon was a serial predator with a
long history of violence against women. In fact, he'd only just been

acquitted of rape two days before he murdered Deana Bowdoin. The magistrate who set him free was Maricopa County Superior Court judge Sandra Day O'Connor, later to become a U.S. Supreme Court Justice. She had found Dixon "not guilty by reason of insanity."

This acquittal is likely what kept Dixon off police radars at the time of the Bowdoin murder. Usually, in cases such as this, investigators will haul in any known sex offender living in the area. The reason that Dixon was overlooked is probably because he wasn't registered with a parole officer at the time and had just recently moved into the neighborhood. Dixon would soon end up in prison anyway, sent down on burglary and assault charges.

But in March 1985, Dixon was back on the streets, out on parole and making up for lost time. On April 2, he ambushed a Northern Arizona University student in the parking lot of the campus, held a knife to her throat and then dragged her to the cover of some trees where he raped her. A few months later, he forced a female jogger from a path, again close to the NAU campus. The woman was subjected to a brutal rape. But then Dixon did a curious thing. He expressed remorse for what he'd done, handed his knife to the victim and told her to cut him. The woman refused. Dixon then told her to get dressed and allowed her to leave.

Remorseful he may have been, but not so remorseful that he was prepared to end his reign of terror. Over the months that followed, Dixon raped at least ten more women. Since rapes often go unreported, the number is likely to be considerably higher. In the end, though, the serial rapist's luck ran out and he was arrested. In 1986, he was convicted on multiple charges and sentenced to life in prison.

By 1996, Clarence Wayne Dixon had spent over a decade behind bars, all the while holding on to his deadly secret. But moves were afoot on the outside, moves that might just expose him for the cold-blooded killer he was, moves that might put him in jeopardy of the death penalty. In Tempe, the Bowdoin case had just been reopened, assigned to cold case investigator, Detective Tom Magazzeni.

Magazzeni began his work with a distinct advantage over the original investigators. They could only have dreamed of the technologies he had at his disposal. DNA profiling was now the go-to method for fingering criminals. The detective wasted little time in submitting the original evidence for testing. Soon he'd have the DNA profile of the killer he was hunting. The only problem was that he had nothing to compare it to.

And so Magazzeni went old school, combing through the list of suspects from the case files, meticulously testing their DNA against the profile he had in his possession. Nothing. The man he wanted wasn't on the list because he'd never been a suspect. It would be five more frustrating years before an advance in computing finally allowed the puzzle pieces to be slotted together. In 2001, the FBI made its CODIS database (Combined DNA Index System) available to state and local law enforcement agencies. Tom Magazzeni could hardly wait to submit his inquiry. It returned a match to an inmate currently serving a life term for multiple sexual assaults.

Twenty-three years had passed since the tragic January night that would be Deana Bowdoin's last on earth. Now, at last, the Tempe police had a name to attach to her murder, the name of Clarence

Wayne Dixon, a 52-year-old former gas station attendant with a penchant for violence against women. It was only now that the police would learn the astonishing truth about Dixon's proximity to Deana at the time of her death. He'd been virtually her neighbor.

Going by Dixon's known M.O., investigators believed that he'd been out trawling that night, looking for a likely victim, when he spotted Deana, returning from the Monastery Bar. The young woman had stopped at the market on her way home and was carrying a carton of milk. Dixon had snuck into the building behind her, lurking in the shadows while she unlocked her front door. He'd then moved in fast, grabbing Deana from behind, forcing her inside and closing the door behind them. After that, Deana would have been at his mercy.

One question remained to be answered. Why had Clarence Dixon killed Deana when he left his other known victims alive? It is probably because the brave young woman resisted him. Dixon was a thug who relied on brute force and a sharp blade to intimidate his victims. But Deana had not been intimidated. She'd put up a fight, refusing to be violated by this man who had forced his way into her world. Some rapists are unsettled by such resistance and will back away from a victim who fights back. Regrettably, Clarence Dixon was not one of those. He was a dyed-in-the-wool misogynist. Deana's refusal to submit only angered him. In the end, it was her bravery that cost her life.

Clarence Wayne Dixon went on trial for murder in November 2007. Found guilty, he was sentenced to death on January 24, 2008, with the jury taking just 20 minutes to reach its decision. He currently awaits execution at the Arizona State Prison in Florence, AZ.

A Kind of Justice

Television has a way of glamorizing things. Take the spate of CSI programming currently streaming into our living rooms. If these are to be believed, then Crime Scene Investigators are all MIT graduates who look like centerfolds and dress, on a cop's salary, in the latest couture. Their cases, most often, are solved by flashes of pure genius. These are the Einsteins of the policing world, wrapped in a package that is Chris Hemsworth or Jennifer Lawrence.

Cold case investigators are similarly misrepresented. According to Hollywood, these are grizzled old pros brought back from pasture to pore over boxes of dusty old evidence hoping for a flash of inspiration. Nothing could be further from reality. While it is true that cold case detectives tend to be among the most experienced of investigators, their cases are most often closed by advances in technology. DNA is the star of the show, of course. A criminal who evaded capture in the '60s or '70s might have thought that he got away with it. Not anymore. The tiniest scrap of biological material, left at a crime scene, decades ago, can now be processed, an incriminating profile extracted. And with recent advances in familial DNA, the net gets cast ever wider.

Given these innovations, it would be fair to ask why we even have cold cases anymore, why we can't just go back and close them all. The answer comes down mainly to two things. The first is that material may not have been collected from the crime scene, may have been contaminated, or may have been destroyed. The second is money. DNA tests are expensive, prohibitively so for smaller departments. It also costs to maintain a squad of detectives focused only on cold cases. For many jurisdictions, hard choices have to be made, and those choices usually come down on the side of more current investigations. Often, the only way that a small department gets to revisit cold cases is through a grant from the National Institute of Justice. In 2012, the Long Beach PD received just such an award. One of the cases that they flagged for review was the 1972 murder of Helen Sullivan.

The grant, in fact, had arrived just in time. Facing a serious budgetary squeeze, the LBPD had started clearing out old case files and destroying old evidence. The clear-out had left them with nearly 900 cold cases still on file, an unmanageable number given their financial constraints. Case files up to the late '60s had already been pulled and evidence discarded. That left the '70s still intact, and that was a good thing. The Sullivan murder was a particularly brutal one. This was a case that investigators were desperate to solve.

It happened in the early morning hours of January 21, 1972. Helen was 54 then, and the mother of three adult children. She was also a hard-working entrepreneur who had started out selling makeup and jewelry and had later become an agent for NutriLite and Amway. Generally, she figured near the top of those companies' sales charts. In fact, she'd been so successful that the profits from her businesses had financed the purchase of a second property.

The Sullivans lived in a small two-bedroom home on the 6600 block of Olive Avenue in North Long Beach. With their children moved out, it was all that they needed. But when the Spanish-style stucco next door came up for sale, Helen put in a bid and bought it outright. At first, her mother lived in the house, but Helen later used it as a base for her business. She was working there early on that Friday morning when her killer found her. Helen's husband, Edward, would arrive home from his shift at the Shell refinery in Wilmington to find her office light still on. He went to check on her and walked in on a scene that would traumatize him for the rest of his days. Helen had been savagely beaten and stabbed to death. The autopsy would reveal that she had also been raped.

This was a difficult crime to solve. The killer had left little evidence at the scene, bar a partial fingerprint. There was also semen, of course, but the technology that would have made this a case-solving piece of evidence was still decades in the future. Back in the day, all that the police could hope for was a blood-type match, which might eliminate a suspect or flag him for further investigation. And that was only if they had someone in custody, which they did not.

Making things even more difficult for Long Beach investigators at that time was the ongoing construction of the Artesia Freeway. The road would cut directly through North Long Beach, and houses that fell in its path had been bought up by the dozen. In January 1972, many of these homes stood empty and boarded up, awaiting demolition. This had attracted vagrants and opportunistic criminals to the area. At the time of Helen Sullivan's murder, her neighborhood had seen a significant uptick in crime. There'd been arrests and several shootouts in which suspects were killed.

The killer of Helen Sullivan, though, would remain stubbornly at large. Or perhaps not. Perhaps he was one of those arrested or killed by law enforcement. That, at least, was what the police told the grieving Sullivan family when it became clear that they were not going to solve Helen's murder. The person who'd done this was probably dead or in jail, they said. Helen's husband and children would have to be satisfied with that. Ed went to his grave never knowing the truth. So, too, did Helen's oldest daughter, Elinor.

But now, forty years on, there was hope at last for Helen's two surviving children. In January 2012, they received a call from Mike Dugan, a retired detective assigned to the LBPD's Cold Case Unit. Their mother's case was being reopened, Dugan told them. Biological material from the original crime scene had already been sent for processing. There was every chance that a DNA match would be returned.

The result wasn't long in coming. The DNA profile had been matched to a man named Emanuel Miller, an ex-con with a criminal record a mile long. Miller had a particular penchant for attacks on women. In fact, he'd been paroled from his latest prison stint just days before Helen Sullivan's murder. A native of Los Angeles, Miller's extensive record did not include a single arrest in Long Beach. Most likely, he'd been drawn to the area for the same reason as others of his ilk. There were plenty of places to hide, plenty of vacant houses where he could set up base and surveil the area. That was probably how he spotted Helen, sitting behind her desk all alone, in an empty house, in the middle of the night. To a predator like Miller, an opportunity like that would have been impossible to turn down.

Forty years on and the Long Beach Police Department had just solved the coldest of cold cases on its books. Unfortunately, there would be no take down, no bringing to justice of a man who deserved to feel the full force of the law. Emanuel Miller was dead and had been for the past 22 years. He'd died in 1990, at the age of 54, while serving yet another jail term.

For Helen Sullivan's surviving daughters, the news that their mother's killer had finally been identified came as a massive relief. Finally, after 40 years, they had closure. And perhaps they were relieved, too, that the killer was dead, that they wouldn't have to come face-to-face with him in a courtroom, that they wouldn't have to go through the ordeal of a trial and all the painful memories that the testimony would resurrect. It wasn't like Miller had gotten away with it. He'd ended up in prison anyway and he'd died there. That, at least, was a kind of justice.

If I Can't Have You

Jason Tibbs

Rayna Rison was 16 years old, a sophomore at La Porte High School in Indiana, a talented musician, a girl with aspirations of becoming a veterinarian. An intelligent and hardworking teen, Rayna held down three part-time jobs and still found time to play in the school band while maintaining excellent academic results. She was an animal lover, and her favorite moments were spent at the Pine Lake Animal Hospital where her duties included cleaning the kennels and walking the dogs. All of this would have been impressive enough. It was more so when you consider Rayna's tragic backstory. From a young age, she'd been sexually molested by a relative.

The pedophile in question was her brother-in-law, Ray McCarty, married to her oldest sister, Lori. The abuse had begun when Rayna was just 11 years old and had persisted for two years. McCarty had warned the terrified child not to say anything, but in 1989, when Rayna was 13, the secret became impossible to maintain. The little girl became pregnant and tearfully informed her parents what had happened. McCarty was arrested and subsequently convicted of child molestation. His punishment for this crime was a ludicrous three years, with the entire sentence suspended. In the meantime, Rayna was put through the ordeal of an abortion. Adding to her anguish was her sister's decision to remain with the man who had raped her.

It is impossible to imagine the impact that all of this must have had on the naïve 13-year-old. But Rayna Rison appears to have been an uncommonly resilient child. Over the next three years, she held her life together, maintained good grades at school, and started planning for the future. Despite her abuse at the hands of Ray McCarty, she even started dating.

One of Rayna's first boyfriends was a kid named Matt Elser, a classmate of hers at La Porte High. He and Rayna dated for a while in 1993 but then broke up. Then they started thinking about getting back together again and agreed to meet up and talk things over. Just after 6:00 p.m. on the evening of Friday, March 26, 1993, Matt pulled his car into the lot of the animal hospital to pick Rayna up. He arrived to find the place locked down for the night and in darkness. Of Rayna, there was no trace.

Matt was understandably upset to be stood up. But the more he thought about it, the less it made sense. It just wasn't like Rayna to blow him off without even a phone call. Something felt off here. Over the next two hours, Matt would swing by the clinic several times, hoping to find Rayna waiting for him in the parking lot. Each time he was disappointed. Eventually, he decided to drive to the Rison residence.

Rayna's father, Ben, was as surprised as Matt by Rayna's no-show. He was also concerned. This wasn't like his daughter. By 10:30 p.m., with

still no sign of Rayna, Ben and his wife decided to drive to the police
station to report her missing. They were told to wait 24 hours before
filing a report. Ben wasn't about to do that. After working the phones
and finding no one who knew where Rayna might be, Ben and his
wife, along with Rayna's younger sister, Wendy, launched their own
search. By the following morning, they were out papering the
neighborhood with fliers. Then, finally, the police got involved and
issued a public appeal for information.

It was this which generated the first lead. Several witnesses had seen
Rayna outside the animal hospital sitting in a car with two young men.
She appeared to be arguing with one of the men in what witnesses
described as a "lover's quarrel." Who was this man? The police
thought that it might be Matt Elser and brought him in for questioning.
The answers he provided seemed to clear him as a suspect.

The next break in the case came the following evening when Rayna's
car was found abandoned on County Road 200 East, about nine miles
from the animal hospital. The hood was up and the keys in the
ignition. Initially, it was thought that Rayna might have had car
trouble, but when an officer turned the key, the vehicle started right
away. That was troubling. Also of concern was Rayna's purse, lying
on the passenger seat. It seemed unlikely that she'd have left it behind.
Not unless she'd been forced from the vehicle. Finally, there was a
potential lead, a man's ring lying in the foot-well. This turned out to
belong to Jason Tibbs, a boy Rayna had once dated.

Brought in for questioning, Tibbs readily admitted that the ring was
his. He told the officers that he and Rayna had dated for six months
when they were in the seventh grade. The relationship had ended

amicably, he said, and he and Rayna had remained friends. When she had recently asked for his help in fixing a problem with her car, he'd readily agreed. While doing the work, he'd taken off his ring and placed it on the seat. He'd forgotten it there. That was how it had ended up inside the vehicle.

The explanation seemed plausible enough. However, the investigators were not ready to let Tibbs off the hook just yet. They wanted to know his whereabouts on the night that Rayna went missing. Tibbs said that he'd been playing a game called "fox hunt" with a group of friends. This is a kind of vehicular hide-and-seek, where the participants drive around in their cars and give clues to their whereabouts via CB radio. Those who played that night remembered Jason being involved at the start of the evening. No one could recall seeing him later on. Still, the police considered his alibi to have been validated.

Over the weeks that followed, the search for Rayna Rison was gradually scaled down. There is only so long that a small town police force can sustain such an undertaking. Then, on April 26, 1993, there was a major turn of events. A fisherman was casting his line at a pond just north of US 20 in La Porte County when he spotted something in the water. It turned out to be a human body, fully-clothed, weighed down by two large logs that had been placed across its back. Rayna Rison had been found.

Even before the autopsy results were released, there could be no doubt that this was a homicide. Rayna's body bore no obvious signs of trauma, but the medical examiner determined that she'd been asphyxiated, most likely by manual strangulation.

It was at this point in the investigation that the police received a valuable lead. An anonymous tipster reported that she'd seen Rayna in conversation with her brother-in-law, Ray McCarty, less than an hour before she disappeared. Brought in for questioning, McCarty readily admitted to the conversation. According to him, he'd been looking at a property for sale on Warren Street, across the road from the animal hospital, when he'd spotted Rayna's car in the parking lot. He'd gone to ask if she knew where Lori was. Rayna had said no and he'd then left. Asked why he hadn't reported this sooner, McCarty said it was because he'd picked up a female hitchhiker later that night and didn't want his wife to find out about it. While this seemed like a tenuous excuse, the police had nothing on McCarty and were forced to let him go. The pool of potential suspects was running dry. The case was going cold.

Eighteen months passed. Then, out of the blue, there was a break. Indiana police pulled over a van driven by a man named Larry Hall, wanted for an attempted kidnapping. Officers then searched the vehicle and found a stack of newspaper clippings relating to the Rayna Rison story. They also found a prescription bottle with the name R. Rison on it. Pressed on this, Hall soon broke down and confessed to abducting and killing Rayna. It appeared that the case had resolved itself. However, Hall's confession would turn out to be false. Tracking his movements, detectives discovered that he'd been in Kentucky on the night that Rayna was killed. The prescription bottle also turned out to be fake.

Larry Hall was off the hook for the Rison murder, but he'd soon be convicted of killing another teen, 15-year-old Jessica Roach. Subsequent inquiries suggested that Hall was a serial killer, responsible for the deaths of up to 40 women. He was sentenced to life in prison with no possibility of parole.

An extremely dangerous man had been taken off the streets. That was a win, but it got the authorities no closer to finding Rayna Rison's killer. In 1998, five years after the murder, La Porte PD decided to take another run at the case. Rayna's pedophile brother-in-law, Ray McCarty, was the primary focus of their investigation. A search warrant was obtained, and when dried blood was found in his car, McCarty was arrested and charged with murder. However, the police were never able to determine the source of the blood or if it was even human. Ray McCarty might have been a despicable human being, but the police did not have the evidence to win a murder conviction against him. He was ultimately released with all charges dropped. The Rison file went back into the cold case section.

Fast forward a decade to 2008. Fifteen years had now passed since Rayna Rison's murder, and the police held out very little hope that her killer would ever be caught. Then, in March 2008, there was another twist. An inmate named Ricky Hammons, jailed on a murder charge, contacted the police and said that he had information relating to the Rison case. According to him, he knew who'd killed Rayna. It was her former boyfriend, Jason Tibbs.

The story that Hammons had to tell seemed incredibly farfetched, like something out of a bad Hollywood movie. He said that Tibbs had been dating his sister at the time and had borrowed her car on the night of the murder. At some point during the evening, the 14-year-old Hammons had gone down to the barn to smoke a joint. He was lurking in the shadows when he heard a car approaching. Concealing himself in the upper loft, he saw his sister's car pull into the barn. Tibbs and another man, Eric Freeman, got out of the vehicle. From his place in the loft, Hammons saw Tibbs pop the trunk, open the lid, and rummage around inside. As he did so, the blankets were moved aside and Hammons saw a face. He hadn't realized that it was Rayna until he saw her story on the news. Even then, he'd decided not to come forward since doing so would get him in trouble for smoking marijuana.

Detectives were extremely skeptical of this story, doubly so, given its source. They had very little to lose by following it up, though, and so they brought Eric Freeman in for questioning. It is unclear what Freeman told the police at this time. Whatever it was, it would be five years before prosecutors were ready to move forward with the case. In 2013, Freeman was presented with a sweetheart deal, full immunity in exchange for his testimony against Jason Tibbs. He accepted in a heartbeat. A few months later, La Porte PD officers took 38-year-old Tibbs into custody and charged him with the murder of Rayna Rison.

The trial of Jason Tibbs eventually got underway in October 2014, a full 21 years after the murder of which he stood accused. Ricky Hammons and Eric Freeman were the chief prosecution witnesses, and what they had to say was devastating to the defense. According to Freeman, Tibbs had been obsessed with Rayna Rison and determined to rekindle their romance. The news that she was about to get back with Matt Elser had sent him into a tailspin. He'd arrived at the animal hospital at around 6:00 p.m. that evening, just as Rayna was leaving work.

Rayna was coaxed into the car to talk. Jason begged her to come back to him, but Rayna was unmoved, telling him that she and Matt had decided to patch things up. That was when Jason got angry and punched her in the face. He then grabbed her and started choking her, strangling her to death right there in the parking lot. Tibbs and Freeman then moved Rayna's body to the trunk and drove to the pole barn to discuss what to do next. They had no idea that Ricky was hiding inside, watching their every move. Later, they drove out to a pond near Range Road and submerged the body, weighing it down with logs. "If I can't have her, then nobody can," Jason told Eric as they drove away.

Jason Tibbs's obsession with Rayna Rison was confirmed via another source, the lovelorn letters he'd written to her in which he'd stated that he would "go to almost any extreme" to be her boyfriend again. It gave credence to Eric Freeman's story and ultimately sealed Tibbs's fate. Found guilty of murder, he was sentenced to 40 years in prison, a sentence that was later upheld by the Indiana Supreme Court.

FOOTNOTE: In February 2018, Ray McCarty was taken into custody on a felony battery charge. A few days later, on February 25, McCarty hanged himself in his cell.

Neighborhood Monster

Gregory Davies

The Melbourne Cup is an institution in Australia. Run every year on the first Tuesday in November, this is more than a horse race. It is a festival, a celebration, a tradition going all the way back to 1861. Australians call it "the race that stops the nation," and they aren't kidding. In the city of Melbourne and in many other parts of Victoria, Cup Day is an official holiday. Elsewhere, the country literally grinds to a halt as eager punters crowd into pubs or sit glued to television sets at work or at home, taking in the iconic event.

Julie Maybury wasn't really a huge horse racing fan. But like all of her countrymen, she was caught up in cup fever on November 6, 1984. That afternoon, Julie convened to her local pub in the Melbourne suburb of Preston, along with her neighbor Lorna Simpson. Also dragged along to watch the race was Julie's daughter, Kylie, a pretty 6-year-old with a boyish bob hairstyle and a spray of freckles across her nose. Kylie was in a bit of a huff that day. She'd wanted to attend a birthday party which her mom had not allowed. Still, even she was caught up in the moment as 10-to-1 shot Black Knight romped to victory and the crowd around her erupted. Kylie was in a much better mood when she left the pub with her mom and Lorna at around 4:30.

After leaving the pub, the trio walked together to Lorna's house, where they'd remain until just after five, when Julie decided that it was time to go home. But then Julie remembered something. She remembered that she'd meant to buy some sugar and had forgotten to do so. Reaching into her purse, she withdrew 90 cents and handed it to Kylie. "Run down to the supermarket and pick up a bag of sugar," she told her daughter. It was a chore Kylie had performed many times before. This time would be her last.

The supermarket in question was just 150 yards away on Plenty Road, a mere five minutes each way for a fleet-footed youngster like Kylie. But as the minutes ticked by with no sign of the little girl, Julie began to become concerned. By 5:40, 25 minutes since Kylie's departure, she was worried enough to go looking. Kylie had definitely made it to the store, a clerk confirmed that. But where was she now? Desperate, Julie and Lorna started walking the streets, questioning passersby. What one of them had to say was deeply concerning. She'd seen a little girl with a bob hairstyle getting into a white Holden station wagon. That was when Julie called in the police.

A search was launched that night, a search that continued into the hours of darkness and found nothing. Then, at 12:45 a.m. came devastating news. An off-duty firefighter had found a child's body lying in a gutter on Tyler Street, in an area the police had previously searched. It was Kylie Maybury. The little girl had been raped and strangled. An autopsy would find traces of the powerful sedative diazepam in her system, suggesting that she had also been drugged. That was perhaps a mercy. Kylie would probably have been unconscious when she was violated and throttled to death.

From the very start of the investigation, the police were convinced that the killer was a local man. The fact that the body had showed up in an area they'd searched just hours before, suggested that it had been hidden somewhere nearby and dragged out after dark when the killer thought it was safe. The police also believed that Kylie must have known her killer since she appeared to have gone with him willingly. That seemed to point to a family friend or a relative. The person who most interested investigators was Kylie's grandfather, John Moss. Moss was subjected to a brutal round of questioning, becoming so despondent that he took his own life in 1985. This tragedy would be compounded two years later, when the investigative team switched its attention to Kylie's uncle, Mark Maybury. He, too, was driven to suicide by the allegations.

There is an old truism in homicide investigations, one that suggests that a murder that goes unsolved in the first 48 hours is likely to remain so. In the age of modern forensics, that belief is probably not as valid as it once was. However, it remains undoubtedly true that time is not the investigator's friend. The further the investigation is from the criminal event, the harder it becomes to resolve it. By the 1990s, the Victoria police were more or less clutching at straws, looking into known pedophiles who may have been in the area of Preston on that Melbourne Cup Day. One who was of particular interest was Robert Arthur Lowe, a convicted child killer and rapist. However, Lowe was cleared when his DNA profile did not match semen retrieved from Kylie's clothing.

Arthur Lowe was not the first sex offender to be questioned regarding the murder of Kylie Maybury, nor would he be the last. The Victoria Police were following a strategy employed by law agencies the world

over, one so cleverly parodied in the movie, *The Usual Suspects*.
When in doubt, haul in everyone known to commit the kind of crime
you're investigating. This makes perfect sense, of course, and in many
cases, it yields results. It would definitely have done so in the Kylie
Maybury case. However, for whatever reason, the police decided to
ignore the obvious suspect sitting right under their noses.

Gregory Keith Davies was 41 years old in 1984, living with his mother
in Preston, just a few houses away from Kylie Maybury. Davies was a
man with a long criminal history. In the 1960s, he'd been given a
suspended sentence for fraud and larceny and had served time for
sexual offenses against children. Then, in February 1971, Davies
attacked a 14-year-old schoolgirl with a hammer and beat her to within
an inch of her life. Arrested for that crime, he admitted that he had
planned on raping the girl. He was subsequently found not guilty of
attempted murder by reason of insanity. Sent to a secure hospital, he
would remain behind bars until November 1982. A short while later,
he arrived in Preston and moved in with his mother. Kylie Maybury,
living less than 100 yards away, was four years old at that time. She
had just two years left to live.

So why wasn't Gregory Davies questioned by the police? As a matter
of fact, he was. Detectives spoke to him just two days after Kylie was
killed. At the time, Davies offered an alibi, which was backed up by
his mother. The police took him at his word. It is uncertain whether
they asked what car he drove. Had they done so, they would have
learned that his ride was a white Holden station wagon.

In 2016, the Victoria police began looking into several old cases, the
murder of Kylie Maybury among them. The Maybury case was

actually a prime candidate for this type of investigation since the police had the killer's semen, which had been retrieved from Kylie's underwear. In order to find a DNA match, several suspects were asked to provide a saliva sample. Gregory Davies, who'd been questioned during the original inquiry, was among them. From the moment that he submitted to a cheek swab, his long flight from justice was effectively over.

Gregory Keith Davies was arrested at his home in Waterford Park in June 2016 and charged with the rape and murder of Kylie Maybury. Now 73 years old, Davies did not deny murder but claimed instead that he did not remember. This is undoubtedly a lie. A killer of this type does not forget the terrible things he has done. He replays them over and over in his mind for his own sick pleasure. In any case, Davis did not waste the court's time by trying to assert his innocence. He entered a guilty plea and accepted the sentence that was handed down to him – life in prison with a minimum of 28 years. He will be eligible for parole in 2045…when he is 101 years old.

And those will be hard years, spent in solitary confinement for his own protection. Pedophiles and child killers are reviled in prison, and Davies's highly-publicized case made him more hated than most. On July 23, 2017, while awaiting trial at Port Phillip Prison, he was attacked by two inmates who held him down and poured scalding hot water over his genitals. Davies suffered severe burns and required skin grafts over 15 per cent of his body. It is hard to feel sympathy.

The Killer Falls

It was the kind of neighborhood where people felt a sense of community, a tree-lined enclave in balmy San Diego that residents were loath to leave. Certainly that was the case with Angela Kleinsorge. She and her husband, Paul, had settled in Morena in the 1940s after emigrating from their native Germany. They'd started a business, Point Loma Nursery, and purchased an attractive single-story home at the corner of Gaines and Colusa Streets, within walking distance of the University of San Diego. Here, they'd raised their children, a boy and a girl, and here Angela had continued to live after Paul's death. At 84, she was a doyen of the neighborhood, an elegant, charming senior who enjoyed tending her garden and could be seen taking her daily walk around the area, always immaculately turned out.

Hedy Kleinsorge, Angela's daughter, had a particularly close bond with her mother. The two of them would speak every day on the telephone, and Hedy would often drop by for a visit. They also had a standing arrangement on Saturdays, when Hedy would arrive to take her mother shopping. On the morning of Saturday, February 29, 1992, though, Hedy was concerned. Her habit was to call her mother before she left home, telling her that she was on her way. Today, three calls had gone unanswered, and Hedy feared that her mom, who'd recently undergone hip surgery, might have suffered a fall. Her anxiety was in no way assuaged when she pulled up in front of the house and saw that the porch light was still on and the blinds still drawn. Angela had always been an early riser. Hedy jogged up the path. She had a key to the house, and now she slotted it into the lock with shaking hands. The moment she crossed the threshold, she was calling out her mother's name. The only response that she got was a deathly silence.

A palpable sense of dread now assailed Hedy. Heart thumping in her chest, she walked down the hall, toward her mother's bedroom, her feet moving almost on auto-pilot. She dreaded what she might find there, but it was far, far worse than she could ever have imagined. One look at the carnage within and Hedy was turning, sprinting from the house, screaming in a primal shriek that was barely recognizable as human.

It was a neighbor who called the police. And since the SDPD's Western Division headquarters was barely a block away, officers were there in mere minutes. They entered the property to find the terrible sight that had so traumatized Hedy Kleinsorge. A woman lay on the floor of the master bedroom clad only in a nightgown, the upper part of her body caked in dried blood. The elderly woman had been stabbed multiple times in the neck, and her throat had been slashed. She had numerous defensive wounds to her hands and arms, indicating that she had tried to fight off her attacker. In the end, it had been to no avail. An autopsy would reveal the motive for this cowardly crime. Before her life was so callously snuffed out, the 84-year-old had been savagely raped.

This was a particularly heinous murder, one that would traumatize the quiet San Diego neighborhood for years to come. Who could have inflicted such violence on a helpless old woman? Was it a burglar? Had Angela caught him in the act and been killed as a result? Might he strike again? Even more frightening was the thought that everyone had on their minds but no one wanted to vocalize. Was Angela's killer from the neighborhood? Was there a monster living among them?

This question, this terrifying, traumatizing question, would linger long on the collective consciousness of Morena's residents. It would linger there because the killer was never caught. Detectives worked the case hard, but the leads were paltry and the suspects few. The killer was either clever or lucky or both. By the time the murder book was finally shelved among the cold cases, he was still at large, his act of cowardice and brutality unpunished.

Ask just about any homicide detective, and they'll tell you about the case that haunts them, the case that they were determined to solve but didn't, the case that keeps them awake at night. For Detective Holly Irwin, it was the murder of Angela Kleinsorge. Det. Irwin had worked the original inquiry but had since been forced to take medical retirement due to an ongoing battle with cancer. Then, with the disease in remission, she'd returned to the force as a reserve detective. With her skill set, she was a perfect fit for the Cold Case team. In the summer of 2016, she got the news she'd been longing to hear. The San Diego D.A. had decided to take another crack at the Kleinsorge case.

Twenty-five years had passed since the night that Angela Kleinsorge was murdered, and technology had not stood still in that time. DNA profiling had been available in the early '90s, but it was still in its infancy. Back then, investigators would require a fresh biological sample and a suspect to compare it to. Now, a profile could be extracted from severely degraded material, and there were databases, most notably CODIS, which held millions of records for comparison. The San Diego Police Department had already submitted their profile, of course. In fact, they'd done so numerous times, without result. But now there was a new kid on the block...familial DNA.

The idea behind familial DNA testing is simple. The perpetrator might not have a profile in the database himself, but he might have a close relative who does. A match could be made in this way, and it would allow investigators to narrow their suspect pool considerably, right down to a few individuals. These individuals could then be asked to submit a sample and could thus be eliminated or confirmed as a suspect. In the Kleinsorge murder, the state database served up a hit, a familial link to a convicted felon who had since died. Further investigation revealed that this man had two siblings, one living, one dead.

The living brother was quickly tracked down, tested and cleared of the murder. That left the remaining brother, Jeffrey Falls, who had been killed in a motorcycle accident in San Diego County back in 2006. It was at this time that the police also made a stunning new discovery. The Falls family had lived directly across the street from Angela Kleinsorge at the time of the murder. That put Jeffrey Falls strongly in the frame. It was time to finally bring this case home.

Finding a sample of Falls's DNA wasn't too difficult. The coroner had taken tissue samples at the time of his fatal accident and now handed these over for testing. It was a match. Angela Kleinsorge's killer had been identified at last. Jeffrey Falls had been 42 years old on the day that he died. That would have made him just 17 years of age on the night that he crept through his elderly neighbor's bedroom window and then raped and killed her. Incredibly, he'd managed to stay out of serious trouble since then, taking his secret to the grave with him. Or so he thought. That terrible secret had now been dragged out into the light. Jeffrey Falls had been exposed for the monster he was.

There are some who might say that Falls evaded justice, that he got away with murder. Angela Kleinsorge's family were not among that number. At a news conference to announce the resolution of the case, Hedy Kleinsorge told the assembled media that she had wondered for years if the killer thought he'd gotten away with murdering her mother, or if he even gave a thought to what he'd done. Now, she no longer had to contemplate these painful thoughts. It was, she said, a bittersweet victory.

Down by the River

Prostitution is a perilous line of work, an occupation that puts its practitioners into contact with the very worst that society has to offer. Prostitutes are frequently required to accompany strangers to remote locales, places where they are at the mercy of anyone inclined to take advantage. It is therefore no surprise that they are the preferred prey of serial killers and other assorted psychos. Their profession makes them uniquely vulnerable, frequently in danger of picking up the wrong man...on the wrong night.

Tracy Beslanowitch probably knew all of this when she embarked on her fledgling career as a sex worker. But what was a 17-year-old to do? The runaway from Spokane, Washington, had no saleable skills, no other way of keeping body and soul together. Besides, Tracy had protection, a boyfriend named Chris who watched her back. During the five months she'd worked the streets of Salt Lake City, Utah, she'd had very little trouble. That run of good fortune would come to a tragic end on December 14, 1995.

Tracy had gone out alone that night; not to trawl for johns, but to pick up something to eat at a local Circle K. That should have taken her maybe twenty minutes, but Chris wasn't unduly alarmed when she failed to return within that time frame. He figured she'd run into someone she knew. She certainly wouldn't be working. Their arrangement was that she'd never go with anyone unless he was close at hand, ready to step in if things went awry. That pact had served them well so far.

However, when Tracy still wasn't home two hours later, Chris did start to worry. It was unlike her to stay out this long without letting him know. And so, Chris pulled on a pair of track pants and walked down to the Circle K, hoping to find Tracy there. When that search came up empty, he returned to their shared motel room and waited. Tracy did not come home that night.

At around 8:40 a.m. the next morning, a rancher was walking with his son along a section of the Provo River that ran through his property, about 45 miles south of Salt Lake City. They were savoring the tranquility of the crisp December morning when their enjoyment was abruptly cut short by a gruesome sight. The nude body of a young woman lay on the riverbank, blood congealed in her dark hair and spattered on her shoulders. The rancher ran immediately to call the police. Soon, the area would be crawling with officers and crime scene technicians.

The young woman was judged to be in her late teens to early twenties. She was naked, and her clothing, bar a pair of socks, had been removed from the scene, most likely by her killer. It meant that the police had no way of identifying her, and she entered the record initially as a Jane Doe. Cause of death was blunt force trauma to the head, delivered by a number of rocks that lay nearby, coated in telltale traces of blood. These were bagged as evidence. They were the only clues that investigators would lift from the scene that day. Their primary focus now was identifying the victim.

And they had one vital lead in that regard. The victim had an identifying mark, a small heart-shaped tattoo under her left breast. This was sketched by a police artist and released to the media in the hope of identifying the Jane Doe. It was a strategy that delivered an almost immediate result. When Chris saw the picture, he immediately contacted the police and told them that the victim was his girlfriend, Tracy.

Brought in for questioning, Chris told the police that his girlfriend's last name was Beslanowitch and that she was originally from Spokane. This allowed a detective to track down her family and then to make the call that every police officer hates making. However, the detective was in for a surprise when he reached Jeff Beslanowitch. His daughter, Tracy, was alive and well in Spokane.

So who was the victim? It was likely Tracy's younger sister, Krystal, Beslanowitch said. He then explained a rather convoluted family history. He was not the biological father of the girls but had been married briefly to their mother in the mid-70s. After the divorce, he had raised Krystal and Tracy as his own. Krystal was the problem child, who had accumulated a record for prostitution, drugs and theft by the time she was 15 and had run away from home half-a-year earlier. She frequently used her sister's ID, her stepfather claimed, to make herself appear older.

So now the police knew the identity of their victim, an important first step in any homicide inquiry. The vast majority of murders are committed by someone known to the victim. In this case, investigators liked the boyfriend, Chris, for the crime. Had he really been unaware of his girlfriend's true identity? It didn't seem likely. Why would she keep it a secret from him? And if he had known, why then had he misidentified the victim? Was it to mislead the investigators?

While detectives mulled over these questions, doubts began to creep in. The most annoying of these was the location of the body. Chris didn't own a car, so how could he have brought Krystal to her place of dying, 45 miles away? And then there was the question of motive. Chris swore to detectives that he'd loved Krystal and would never have harmed her. While that might have been a stretch for them to believe, Chris did have every reason to keep her alive. Krystal was the sole breadwinner in the relationship. Chris was financially dependent on her. Why would he eliminate his source of income?

Despite these doubts, Chris would remain at the top of the suspect list. The police also had another potential suspect, a taxi driver named Herb Fry. Fry sometimes drove the local working girls to their appointments, but he had a particular thing for Krystal. He'd told several people that he was in love with her and that "if I can't have her, nobody can." So had Fry told Krystal about his feelings? Had she laughed him off? Had he killed her in a fit of rage? It was an interesting theory. Unfortunately, there was not a shred of actual evidence to support it. Despite the tireless work of Salt Lake City detectives, the case went cold.

DNA profiling was already a decade old at the time Krystal Beslanowitch was murdered. It had already been used to resolve some sensational cases, most notably that of British serial killer, Colin Pitchfork. But the technology was still rather primitive back then. When forensic scientists ran tests on the rocks from the Beslanowitch crime scene back in 2008, they were able to extract Krystal's DNA profile and the partial profile of an unknown male. This was insufficient as a means of identification, but it could be used to eliminate suspects or keep them under suspicion. When the partial profile was compared to that of Krystal's former boyfriend, Chris, the result was negative. Ditto Herb Fry. The suspect list had just been reduced to zero.

And so, the killer of Krystal Beslanowitch, whoever he was, remained at large. In truth, he was living on borrowed time. Technology stands still for no man, and in a field as important as DNA profiling, there is plenty of funding to grease the wheels of progress. The next few years saw the invention of a groundbreaking extraction tool known as the M-Vac. This is basically a compact vacuum system which sprays micro-jets of a sterile solution onto a surface and then hoovers up the liquid along with any biological material that is present. It allows for the collection of truly microscopic samples for processing, samples up to 90% smaller than was previously possible. In 2013, Salt Lake City PD decided to apply the M-Vac to its primary evidence, the rocks that had been used to club Krystal Beslanowitch to death.

The tests were performed by Sorenson Forensics, a private DNA-testing company often used by Utah's law enforcement agencies. And the results were spectacular. A full profile was extracted. This was then run against the CODIS database and delivered a match. The DNA was from a long-haul trucker named Joseph Michael Simpson, a man who already had a murder conviction to his name. Back in 1987,

Simpson had stabbed a man to death. He'd been convicted of second-degree murder but had served less than eight years for the crime. At the time of Krystal Beslanowitch's murder, he was living in Clearfield, a short drive from Salt Lake City.

Simpson wasn't difficult to find. He was traced to Sarasota, Florida, where he was still plying his trade as a truck driver. The temptation must have been to pull him in for questioning immediately, but investigators wanted to be absolutely certain that he was their man before making their move. A team of Wasatch County investigators was thus dispatched to Florida, where they tailed Simpson for days before obtaining a discarded cigarette butt. DNA was extracted from the filter and run against the sample obtained via the M-Vac. It was a match. Joseph Michael Simpson had evaded justice for 18 years. Now his time was up.

Taken into custody, Simpson waived extradition and was brought back to Utah to face trial. The defense he offered was never likely to succeed. According to Simpson, he'd paid Krystal for sex on the night that she died but had left her alive and unharmed. His theory was that someone else had then picked her up and killed her.

This quite ludicrous story might have had some merit had the murder weapon not been retrieved from the crime scene. How did Simpson explain his DNA on the rock that had caved in Krystal Beslanowitch's skull? He couldn't, and with that, his case was sunk. Simpson made an impassioned plea for leniency during the sentencing phase of the trial, begging the judge not to deny him the possibility of one day obtaining his freedom. Like the pleas that his victim had probably uttered in her final moments, his would fall on deaf ears. In September 2016, he was sentenced to life in prison with no possibility of parole. But for the genius invention that is the M-Vac, he would likely have escaped justice.

Robert Keller

A Bullet for Your Broken Heart

Ask anyone about Roy Joe McCaleb and they'd tell you that he was a solid guy, a good guy, a man you could rely on. They'd also tell you that the 51-year-old construction foreman had been handed a rough hand in recent times. First, his wife had walked out, ending their 22-year marriage. Then his daughter was diagnosed with Friedreich's Ataxia, a debilitating neurological disease that would claim her life in 1980, at the age of just 23. Joe Roy had barely recovered from that body blow when he was struck by another. His son had the same disease, and it was progressing quickly, confining him to a wheelchair in just a couple of months. It was as though a vengeful God had suddenly taken an intense dislike to Roy Joe McCaleb.

But then, in 1983, an angel appeared on Roy Joe's horizon. Her name was Carolyn, and she worked in the accounts department at Brown & Root, the Houston construction firm where Roy Joe had spent the last 20 years of his working life. Carolyn was 41 years old and recently divorced. She was pretty and she was fun to be with. Roy Joe fell quickly and he fell hard. In no time at all, he'd asked Carolyn to be his bride.

Roy Joe McCaleb was nobody's fool. That's another thing his friends
would have told you about him. But love can deprive even the most
rational among us of our good judgement. Perhaps Roy should have
paid better attention to his ladylove's checkered past in the marital
stakes. On the day that Carolyn waltzed down the aisle with him, she
had already made the trip five times before. Each of those unions, bar
the last, had ended in divorce. That last marriage, to a man named
Melvin Laxson, had not yet been dissolved when she wed Roy Joe.

And yet, for all the intrigue that accompanied it, the union between
Carolyn and Roy Joe appeared to be a happy one. The pair shared a
love of Big Band music from the 1940s, and they had a regular card
game with a couple named LeBlanc who they visited often. According
to Mary LeBlanc, they appeared to be very much in love. The only
dark cloud was Carolyn's aversion to Roy Joe's disabled son. She took
an instant dislike to the young man, making him feel so unwelcome
that he eventually moved out. Carolyn then allowed her own son to
take up residence, along with his girlfriend. Both were present in the
house on the night of September 22, 1985, the night that disaster was
visited yet again upon Roy Joe McCaleb.

An intruder entered the McCaleb property that night and used a .38
Special to pump two bullets into Roy Joe's forehead as he lay
debilitated in his bed, recovering from a recent back surgery. Carolyn
then engaged the intruder in a life-and-death struggle during which he
dropped the revolver. Picking it up, she fired two shots at the retreating
form and missed. That, at least, was the story that she told the police.

This "mystery intruder" storyline has been a standby in domestic shootings since forever. In fact, it is so commonplace that it formed the basis of the 1963 TV series, *The Fugitive* (later a Hollywood blockbuster starring Harrison Ford). In the cinematic version, the lead character, Dr. Richard Kimble, was telling the truth despite evidence suggesting otherwise. In the case of Carolyn McCaleb, the Houston police had their doubts. Several things about the shooting just didn't add up.

According to Carolyn's account, she'd locked the front and back doors of the house that night and couldn't understand how the intruder had entered the property. The police couldn't understand that either. There was no sign of a break-in. Then Carolyn said that the intruder had attacked her with a wire coat hanger, inflicting several scratches. The scratches were there alright, and the police bagged the hanger as evidence. Submitted to forensic tests, it came back negative for human blood or cellular matter.

As for the shooting itself, Carolyn said that the man had run toward the master bedroom where her husband was sleeping. She kept a revolver there, tucked under her pillow. Somehow, the intruder had located it right away, leveled it at Roy Joe and pulled the trigger. Carolyn had then entered the room and wrestled the gun from him, firing after him as he fled. Oddly, Carolyn's son and his girlfriend had heard nothing of the struggle. They'd only been alerted when they heard gunshots.

And the forensics in this case also raised questions. In Carolyn's version of events, she had not been in the room when Roy Joe was shot. How then did she have blood-spatter on her nightdress? And why had she been in such a hurry to take a shower, disobeying a direct instruction from the responding officers? Was it to destroy forensic evidence? The police believed so.

Finally, there was the issue of motive. Why would a total stranger break into a suburban home and gun down the householder without provocation? The answer, according to Carolyn, was simple. The intruder wasn't a stranger. She'd encountered him several days earlier, in equally terrifying circumstances. On that occasion, he'd carjacked her, dragged her from her vehicle and subjected her to a brutal rape. She hadn't reported this to the police, she said, because her husband was recuperating from surgery and she didn't want to upset him. Now she regretted her silence. Quite obviously, the man had found out where she lived and come back to silence her. Except that it was Roy, and not she, who'd paid the price.

This story, too, sounded like a wild fabrication to the police. It was also full of contradictions. At first, Carolyn described the rapist as a white man. In a later telling, she said he was black. Confronted with this contradiction, Carolyn doubled down on her story and affirmed that her attacker had been African-American. She'd lied at first, she claimed, because she was ashamed of being raped by a black man. This about turn only threw further doubt on her fantastical tale.

In fact, investigators had by now uncovered a far more compelling motive. Carolyn had recently taken out a couple of life insurance policies on her husband, to a total value of $198,000. She stood to benefit handsomely from his death.

All of the evidence, the lies, the anomalies, seemed to point the finger of suspicion at one person – the not-so-grieving widow, Carolyn McCaleb. But suspicion is one thing, proof another. The D.A. did not believe that the case was winnable. As outlandish as the intruder story was, any half-competent defense attorney could make an argument for reasonable doubt. Juries have been swayed by less.

And so, Carolyn was off the hook, at least for now. Getting her hands on her windfall, though, would prove more difficult. The D.A.'s office had informed the insurance companies that this was an ongoing murder inquiry with Carolyn as the chief suspect. The result was a protracted court battle which was finally settled when Carolyn received a fraction of the policy value, just $19,000. It barely covered her attorney's fees. In the meantime, the widow McCaleb had other legal problems to worry about. In 1986, she was arrested and charged with bigamy. The charges would later be dropped.

The murder inquiry, likewise, was going nowhere. With no new evidence, it had stalled, with little chance of a resolution. The only reason it remained on the Houston PD radar at all was because of the regular calls made to the department by Roy Joe's daughter. Pam Nalley was determined to see her father's killer brought to justice. In 2008, it seemed that she would finally get her wish. Carolyn, since remarried and divorced again, was arrested and charged with Roy Joe McCaleb's murder.

The case, though, would never make it before a jury. At the arraignment, Carolyn's lawyer argued that too much time had passed; that witnesses (including Roy Joe's son) had died; that no new evidence had been uncovered. If the state had been unable to make its case back in 1985, why would it be any different now? Judge Kevin Fine agreed and dismissed the charges. The case would lay fallow for five more years before the D.A. was ready to try again.

Much had happened in the intervening years. The defendant, now going by the name Carolyn Krizan-Wilson, was 71 years old and suffering from early stage Alzheimer's. She'd also had a change of heart. Now she was ready to talk and admit her role in Roy Joe McCaleb's death. There had been no carjacking, no rape, no intruder. Carolyn had been the one who'd pulled the trigger, standing over her husband and executing him while he slept. She'd done it for one of the oldest reasons in the book – money.

Carolyn's punishment for this callous crime was a ridiculously light sentence of just six months in prison plus ten years of "deferred adjudication." Her time would be served at the Harris County Jail. But no sooner had she started her sentence than she was casting doubt on her guilt. Now she was claiming that she was actually innocent and that she had only confessed to put the case behind her. "She's just tired of it all," her lawyer informed the media.

No one, least of all Roy Joe's kin, believed Carolyn's protestations. To them, this was a just another lie, in a long line of deceptions. Their father's killer was behind bars, albeit for the briefest of jail terms. That felt like a vindication. After 30 long years, there was justice for Roy Joe at last.

The Other Ripper

Christopher Smith

Between the years 1975 and 1980, the English counties of Yorkshire and Lancashire were terrorized by a brutal serial killer. Peter Sutcliffe, better known by his chilling epithet, the Yorkshire Ripper, would murder 13 women, butchering them with a depravity not seen since the original Ripper stalked the streets of Whitechapel in the 1880s. Like Jack, Sutcliffe preyed primarily on sex workers, although he wasn't exclusive in this regard. Any woman who crossed his path in a sufficiently secluded area was at risk of a horrible death.

Joan Mary Harrison wasn't a prostitute, at least not in the common application of the word. The 26-year-old did sleep with men, but she never solicited cash payment and had never been arrested for solicitation. Her recompense usually took the form of booze or drugs or a place to crash for the night. Joan's life, though, was a train wreck. Addicted to drugs, alcohol, and over-the-counter cough syrup; spending most of her nights trawling the pubs of Preston's notorious 'Skid Row'; crashing in filthy squats and doss houses and sometimes even passing out on the sidewalk or in alleyways, Joan seemed to be riding the fast train to oblivion. It hadn't always been that way. There had been a time when Joan Harrison, nee Riding, was a devoted, house-proud mother-of-two.

Born and raised in Chorley, Lancashire, Joan had graduated from St Mary's School in that town. She'd married young, later moving to Preston with her husband. Over the first few years, the union would be blessed with two daughters, Maxine and Denise. But by then, the marriage was already in trouble, much of it related to Joan's prodigious appetite for booze. She and her husband eventually split, and Joan then shacked up with a man named Wilf Roach, who was 12 years her senior. At just 22, she had already started her descent into alcoholism. That, combined with her accelerating drug use and casual promiscuity, eventually led to Roach jumping ship as well.

Alone and living on benefits, Joan's life continued its downward spiral. In no time at all, she lost her house to the bank and her daughters to social services. Then, just when things appeared to be at their lowest ebb, a white knight appeared. Paul Harrison was a hardworking carpet-fitter from Preston. He would become the second man to march Joan down the aisle but, like his predecessor, he was no match for her appetites. Unable to cope with his wife's heavy drinking and drug use, Paul threw in the towel and moved on. As low as her life had been to this point, Joan now descended to an even deeper level of desperation. On many nights, she could be found at a derelict property in Avenham, a place frequented by winos and addicts. Here, she'd drink herself into a stupor on whatever she could lay her hands on – cheap wine, gin, cider, even methylated spirits. The means didn't matter. All that mattered was the buzz.

Joan's family tried to rescue her from this terrible plight, of course they did. But as anyone who has a junkie for a relative will tell you, that path is fraught with frustration. When her sister offered her a place to stay, Joan thanked her by stealing £50 from her purse. She also stole a doctor's prescription, which she altered to increase the quantity of prescribed pills. That saw her arrested and hauled before the Preston Magistrates Court in 1974, on a day that also happened to be her 25th birthday.

One year later, on the morning of October 30, 1975, police in Leeds were called to the site of a particularly brutal murder. Wilma McCann, a prostitute and mother of four young children, had been beaten to death with a hammer, stabbed several times in the throat and abdomen with what appeared to be a screwdriver. It was an incredibly savage attack but perhaps not unexpected. Prostitute murders are a regrettably frequent occurrence. What the police didn't know at that time was that this one was different. The Yorkshire Ripper had just announced his deadly presence.

Less than three weeks on from the murder of Wilma McCann, on Thursday, November 20, 1975, Preston would have its own 'Ripper-style' murder. Joan Harrison had worked an early shift at St Mary's Hostel that day, earning a few pounds by washing plates and doing some general cleaning. Finishing up around lunchtime, she and some colleagues convened to a nearby pub where Joan soon burned through her earnings. She was later seen scrounging drinks at several pubs in the New Hall Lane area. Still later, she showed up at St Mary's Hostel, slightly drunk and needing some shuteye. She departed about an hour later, heading for a house in Deepdale, where she was living at the time with a man named David Keighley.

But by now, Joan's booze-buzz was wearing off. She needed another drink, and so she left again, heading out into the drizzly night. Some ten minutes later, at around 10:30 p.m., she was spotted on Church Street, in the town center. She was dressed in brown calf-length boots and a green three-quarter length coat with an imitation fur collar. This was the last time that anyone, bar her killer, saw Joan Harrison alive.

Mildred Atkinson had a Sunday routine which always involved an early morning walk to the shops to buy the newspaper. The 47-year-old was doing just that on November 23. She was following her regular route, passing by a disused lock-up garage on Berwick Road when a gust of wind blew the door open. What Mildred saw inside those squalid quarters would live with her for the rest of her days. There was a body on the ground, partially covered by a tatty green coat. A pool of blood spread out from around the body. There would be no Sunday papers today. Mildred immediately rushed home to call the police.

Joan Harrison had been killed in a way that was startlingly similar to Wilma McCann, 70 miles away in Leeds. Her killer had launched a frenzied attack, bludgeoning her to death with a hammer. He'd also bitten her on the left breast, breaking the skin with his teeth. He'd then arranged the body in what the police called a 'ritualistic fashion'. Then he'd covered her with her coat and disappeared into the night. He had, however, left behind a vital clue. He'd had sex with Joan before she died. Semen was retrieved from her corpse. It would be tested as blood group B.

The inquiry into Joan Harrison's death was hampered from the start by a lack of reliable witnesses. Most of Joan's associates were drunks and drug addicts with addled memories. Constructing a reliable timeline of the murdered woman's movements would prove impossible. As is always the case in inquiries such as this, Joan's lovers, past and present, came under suspicion. David Keighley and Wilf Roach were both questioned and subsequently cleared by alibi and by a saliva test. As the police became increasingly desperate, they even questioned Joan's brother, Bill. He too was cleared. Despite the best efforts of an 80-strong squad of detectives, a year passed, then two, then three. The case was going nowhere.

Meanwhile, 70 miles to the northeast of Preston, the aforementioned Yorkshire Ripper was cutting a deadly swathe. By March 1978, he had already claimed seven victims, easily evading the bumbling police force and throwing the entire country, particularly the Northeast, into panic. The Ripper had strayed from his home turf by now, killing 20-year-old Jean Jordan in Manchester in October 1977. And yet the murder of Joan Harrison, which bore so many similarities to his other crimes, was not considered part of the series. That is to say, it wasn't considered part of the series until the letter arrived on the desk of West Yorkshire Constabulary's assistant chief constable, George Oldfield.

With the benefit of hindsight, we know that the missive (and the ones to follow) were sent by a hoaxer. Nonetheless, the writer made a clear reference to the Joan Harrison murder. "Up to number eight," he boasted. "Now you say seven but remember Preston 75." He would later repeat this claim in a letter to the Daily Mirror newspaper. Later still, he would deluge the Ripper task team with tape recordings, sending them off on a wild goose chase that seriously hampered the investigation.

Whether or not the police ever regarded Joan Harrison as a Yorkshire Ripper victim is unclear. Given the credence that they seemed to attach to the hoax letters, it is likely that they did. And one can hardly blame them for reaching that conclusion. There were startling similarities. Joan's killer belonged to the rare blood group B secretor. So, too, did the person who'd written the Ripper letters. The 'ritual elements' that the police had previously alluded to involved taking off Joan's boots and placing them on her thigh. The Ripper had arranged bodies in similar fashion. The bite mark to Joan's breast was just like the one inflicted on Josephine Whitaker. Her abdominal injuries were similar to those found on Jayne MacDonald. The use of a hammer was a Ripper trademark.

All of these similarities might have led the police to the conclusion that Joan Harrison had been killed by the Yorkshire Ripper while on one of his infrequent excursions from his home patch. In fact, the Lancashire Evening Post stated this as fact in a 1979 editorial and even got a senior police officer to admit, on the record, that it was likely.

But the Post, and the police, and the hoax letter writer were all wrong. Peter Sutcliffe had not murdered Joan Harrison. That much would become clear after he was finally captured in 1981. Sutcliffe spoke openly, even boastfully, about the women he'd slaughtered. But he denied having anything to do with Joan's murder. Blood typing would soon clear him anyway. Sutcliffe's blood group was B. Joan's killer was a B secretor, a much rarer type.

And so Joan Harrison's case remained open, even as the police were able to close the files on the 13 murders attributed to Peter Sutcliffe.

Barring a miracle, there seemed very little prospect of ever solving it. In 2008, that miracle happened.

That was when police in Leeds pulled over a 60-year-old man named Christopher Smith for driving erratically. Found to be over the legal alcohol limit, Smith was arrested at the scene. He was later bailed, but not before he was required to provide a DNA sample. That sample was then added to the national database and immediately returned a hit – to an unsolved homicide from 1975. Joan Harrison's killer had finally been found

Regrettably, Christopher Smith would never stand trial for murder. He died of natural causes six days after his DUI arrest. A check on his police record showed that he had previous convictions – for assault and theft and sexual offenses. However, he appeared to have turned over a new leaf in later life and had managed to stay out of trouble for the last 20 years. By remaining on the right side of the law, he'd managed to keep his DNA from entering the system.

But Christopher Smith was undoubtedly the killer of Joan Harrison. Lest there be any doubt, Smith left behind a three-page letter in which he expressed the need to unburden himself of the guilt he'd carried around for "over 20 years." He did not mention Joan by name, but the allusion is clear, given that his semen was found on her corpse. After 35 years, the case file could finally be closed.

FOOTNOTE: John Humble, the writer of the 'Ripper letters,' was eventually apprehended in 2006. He entered a guilty plea to the charge of perverting the course of justice and was jailed for eight years. Peter

Sutcliffe, the real Yorkshire Ripper, died behind bars in November 2020 from COVID-19 related symptoms.

Cage for a Killer

Matthew Breck

If there was one word that friends and neighbors would have used to describe 10-year-old Anna Palmer, that word would have been "joyful." The little girl was friendly and outgoing, with a large circle of friends in her Salt Lake City neighborhood. Her mother, Nancy, called her a "little socialite" who loved life and just couldn't get enough of people. So when Anna called her mom at work on the afternoon of September 10, 1998, and asked if she could go outside to play with some local kids, Nancy said yes. The area where they lived was safe and it was broad daylight. Besides, Nancy had briefed Anna frequently on personal safety – don't talk to strangers; don't get into a car with someone you don't know; always be aware of your surroundings. Nancy was confident that her daughter understood these rules. Her only stipulation on this particular day was that Anna should be indoors by the time she got home from work.

Nancy Palmer was a little later than usual that day, pulling her car into the drive just before seven. She then crossed the lawn and started towards the house. That was when she spotted her daughter lying on the porch and her life, as she knew it, ended. Nancy immediately broke into a run, flew up the steps and dropped into a crouch beside the child. Anna was still, unmoving, her complexion deathly pale. That was concerning enough, but it was the puddle of blood, emanating from a terrible neck wound that sent Nancy into a panic. Feeling for a pulse and finding none, the desperate mother fumbled for her phone and called 911. The dispatcher assured her that units were on the way and told her to start CPR. Nancy followed the instructions to the letter, but she knew, in her heart of hearts she knew, that it was too late. Her little girl, the light of her life, was gone, taken in the cruelest possible way.

The murder of little Anna Palmer was a particularly horrific crime. The ten-year-old had been savagely beaten, brutally stabbed. Five horrible wounds had been inflicted to her throat, running so deep that her spinal cord had been severed. An autopsy would also reveal the probable motive for the attack. Anna had been sexually assaulted. What kind of a monster would do such a thing?

Salt Lake City PD did not know the answer to that question, but they were determined to find out. Officers were flooded into the area, lighting up the night with the red and blue roof lights of their cruisers. Meanwhile, a police helicopter hovered overhead, its high beam scanning the darkened streets below. As CSIs started processing the crime scene, detectives and uniformed officers got to work, going door to door. Had anyone seen anything? Heard anything? Had there been anyone acting suspiciously in the neighborhood?

As it turned out, there had been such an individual. Anna's friend, Loxane Konesavanh, told police about a man who had followed them from the park that afternoon, a creepy-looking individual with a shaved head and a goatee beard. According to Loxane, the man was young, perhaps an older teenager. He was wearing an unbuttoned baseball shirt and had two tattoos on his chest. Another friend of the girls, Amie Johnson, reported that she too had seen this man and that he'd "creeped her out." However, by the time that Anna and Loxane headed towards their respective homes, the man was nowhere to be seen. The girls had exchanged a hug on the corner of 300 East and Bryan Avenue and parted ways there. It was the last time that Loxane would see her friend alive.

This stranger, who had so frightened the little girls, would later be spotted by a neighbor, lurking in an alleyway close to the Palmer residence. That made him the prime suspect, but despite the concerted efforts of police; despite a $11,000 reward for information; despite appeals in the media by Anna's distraught family, he would escape the dragnet. Thousands of man hours, hundreds of interviews, dozens of suspects, all came to nothing. The case that the police were so desperate to solve began to lose momentum. Eventually, it sputtered to a halt.

CODIS (or the Combined DNA Index System, to give it its full title) is a network of electronic databases. As the name suggests, it stores DNA profiles, profiles obtained from crime scenes, from convicted felons, from missing persons. First established in 1990, it has become an invaluable investigative tool for law enforcement agencies across the country. Any unknown profile entered into the database will find a match, if one exists. Even if it doesn't, there might well be a match in the future, since the database is constantly being updated.

Of course, obtaining a DNA profile requires biological material – blood, semen, saliva, hair, or the like. In the Palmer case, the sample that investigators were able to lift was from skin cells found under the victim's fingernails. Little Anna had been desperate to live and had fought hard for her life. In the course of the struggle, she had scratched her attacker. Now, eleven years on, she would reach out from beyond the grave to point the finger of guilt at the man who'd killed her. A DNA profile was extracted from the skin cells found under Anna's fingernails; it was submitted to CODIS and it returned a match. The man who had ended Anna Palmer's life was named Matthew Breck.

A native of California, Breck had come to Utah in 1998, along with his brother Tom. They'd made the journey at the behest of Tom's friend, Todd Clark, who'd told them that there was plenty of work to be found in the Salt Lake City area. But Matt had little interest in gainful employment. His days were spent wandering the streets, getting drunk and committing petty crimes. A wannabe tough guy, he seldom went anywhere without a knife in his pocket. Frequently, he got into fights. In fact, he'd end up in jail just days after Anna Palmer's murder for just such an incident. Facing a long prison term if convicted, Breck had pled down to a misdemeanor and been released with time served. Thereafter, he left Utah and headed north, settling eventually in Idaho.

But Breck's anti-social behavior saw barely any improvement in his new home. In 1999, he was convicted on a burglary charge, serving two years before his release in 2001. A short while later, he was picked up again, this time for committing sodomy on a child under 16. Conviction in that case landed him with a lengthy term at the Idaho Correctional Institution, Orofino. Now a convicted felon, he was required by law to provide a DNA sample. Once his profile was entered into CODIS, it was only a matter of time before his past caught up with him.

It is a moot point whether criminals truly understand the power of DNA profiling. Faced with the evidence against him, Breck fell back on a common strategy – denial. He admitted that he'd been living in Salt Lake City at the time of the murder but denied that he was the person responsible. Presented with a picture of Anna Palmer, he insisted that he'd never seen her in his life. How then had his skin cells ended up under her fingernails on the day she died? Breck couldn't say. He was arrested in the prison interview room and charged with murder. Soon proceedings would be underway to extradite him to Utah.

Twenty-eight states in the nation have the death penalty on their statute books. Utah is one of them, and if ever there was an individual deserving of that sanction, it was Matthew Breck. Certainly, the good people of Salt Lake City would have liked to have seen him ushered out from this world. Sensing the mood and perhaps finally appreciating the potency of the evidence against him, Breck asked for a deal. Taking the life of a child might have come easy to him, but he was desperate to hold on to his own. In 2011, he admitted to the murder of Anna Palmer and accepted a sentence of life in prison without parole. Anything to avoid a death sentence.

Matthew Breck will spend the rest of his natural life behind bars. And that life will not be easy. Child killers are generally reviled in prison, their lives under constant threat from other inmates. Breck will probably be kept in protective custody, removed from the general population. This is an isolated existence, a miserable existence, spent mostly in a concrete box, six feet by eight, a cage for a killer. On his darkest days, Matthew Breck will probably wish that he'd let justice run its course.

Simple Twist of Fate

The year was 1983, and in Los Angeles, California, Elaine Graham was living the life of her dreams. The attractive 29-year-old was married to a man she loved, she had a beautiful two-year-old daughter, she was studying for a degree at California State University Northridge. This latter pursuit meant that Elaine had to employ the services of a babysitter, but she'd found an excellent minder, someone who adored little Elyse and was loved by her in turn. On the morning of March 17, 1983, Elaine followed her usual routine, dropping Elyse at the babysitter before heading for the CSUN campus. It was a beautiful early spring day. It would end in terror.

Elaine never attended classes that day, and she never returned to pick up her daughter. When the alarm was raised, the police quickly launched a search and found her 1971 Volkswagen abandoned in the parking lot of the Santa Ana Fashion Square Mall. The vehicle held an ominous clue. The driving position had been adjusted for someone much taller than Elaine. Clearly someone else had been behind the wheel of the car.

Over the days and weeks that followed, the search for the missing woman continued without success. No one appeared to have seen her or noticed anything untoward on the day she went missing. Then, at last, the police had a clue. A woman called in to offer up a name, Edmond Jay Marr. According to the tipster, Marr's own sister suspected that he might be involved. This seemed rather tenuous, but as detectives started looking at Marr, they began to sit up and take notice. Their suspect was 25 years old and had just been dishonorably discharged from the US Army. He'd been in Northridge visiting his mother on the day that Elaine Graham went missing and had showed up later that day at his sister's residence, which was only a few blocks from the CSUN campus. That put him in the vicinity of a possible abduction.

Edmond Jay Marr looked like a tantalizing prospect, although the police had nothing on him that would amount to probable cause for an arrest warrant. But then Marr played right into their hands by getting himself nabbed for robbery on April 22, 1983. Marr was in possession of a rucksack when he was arrested, and this was found to contain a large, double-edged dagger. Questioned about Elaine Graham, he denied knowing her or having anything to do with her disappearance. With no evidence to prove otherwise, the police were forced to let the matter drop.

Eight months passed. Then, in November 1983, a group of hikers was walking a trail at Brown's Canyon, just outside of Chatsworth, when they came upon a near-complete human skeleton. Dental records would soon reveal the identity of the victim. Elaine Graham had been found. A forensic examination would later identify telltale notches on the bones, suggesting that she had been stabbed to death. But could those notches have been inflicted by the dagger retrieved from number one suspect, Edmond Marr? A forensic specialist said yes. The knife was then dismantled, with the wooden handles removed. Trapped underneath were tiny traces of dried blood. Submitted for a serology test, this returned the result investigators had expected. It was the same blood type as Elaine Graham. The investigative team also subsequently learned that Edmond Marr was very familiar with the area where the body had been found. He'd often hiked Brown's Canyon as a teenager.

All of this added up to a strong circumstantial case, strong enough, investigators believed, to convict Marr. Unfortunately, the LA County District Attorney's Office disagreed. The DA was probably right in this instance. Any half-decent defense attorney could win this on reasonable doubt. And if Marr walked, then that was it. He could not be tried again. He'd have gotten away with murder. Detectives Paul Tippin and Leroy Orozco were understandably disappointed by the decision, but to them, the DA offered some prophetic words of consolation. "Let's wait until technology catches up with this."

Over the next 18 years, the murder book on Elaine Graham lay dormant with the LAPD. Elyse Graham, the two-year-old whose mother had been so cruelly taken from her, was now a young adult who knew her mom only from photographs. Dr. Stephen Graham was still without justice for his murdered wife. Then, to little fanfare, in November 2001, an event occurred that would change the course of myriad criminal investigations. The LAPD announced the formation of its Cold Case Homicide Unit (CCHU).

Operating within the LAPD's Robbery-Homicide Division, the CCHU is the very definition of the overworked and understaffed police department. There are just six investigators assigned to the team, working a caseload of over 8,000 unsolved homicides. So how does one prioritize? Well, one way is to look at the available evidence. Which cases are the most solvable? Another is to listen to submissions from colleagues. In the Graham case, there were Detectives Tippin and Orozco, both since retired but still desperate to see the cold-hearted killer of Elaine Graham brought to justice.

Thus it was that the Elaine Graham murder inquiry was one of the first to be reopened by the CCHU. Detectives Rick Jackson and Tim Marcia were assigned and were impressed by the wealth of evidence the original investigators had gathered. Key among this was the blood evidence. Back in 1984, a serology test had affirmed that the retrieved blood was the victim's type. Now, of course, investigators could determine far more than that. The DA's prophetic words about waiting for technology to catch up had come to pass. A DNA test would determine once and for all whether the blood on Edmond Marr's knife was a match to Elaine Graham.

But there was a problem. Although the lab was able to extract a full DNA profile from the dried blood, there was nothing to compare it to, no biological sample from the victim. It was at this point that Elyse Graham was called upon to contribute to the capture of her mother's killer. Elyse happily gave up blood and saliva, and a familial match was established. The blood on the knife was Elaine's, and the person who owned that knife had killed her. After two decades, Edmond Marr's time was up.

Edmond Jay Marr was arrested and charged with first-degree murder on February 13, 2003. He denied the charges and kept up that stance right until the eve of jury selection when his attorney reached out to the prosecutor and asked for a deal. Marr would plead guilty to second-degree murder and offer a full confession. Since a second-degree conviction carries the same minimum term as first-degree murder (the only difference is in parole requirements), the prosecution agreed.

The confession offered by Edmond Marr would present a haunting glance at the cruel hand of fate, where a couple of minutes either side of the event might have averted a tragedy and spared Elaine Graham's life. According to Marr, the abduction and murder was not planned. He was in a foul mood that day, still fuming over his ejection from the military as he crossed the parking lot at CSUN, on his way to his mother's house. At just that moment, Elaine Graham had the misfortune of pulling up in front of him and getting out of her car. Marr had decided on a whim to kidnap her. He'd forced her back into the vehicle at gunpoint, then told her to drive. That harrowing journey had brought them to Brown's Canyon, an area he knew well. Here, he'd told Elaine to get out and ordered her along the path for about a quarter-mile. At this location, he told her to remove her blouse and then "lost his cool" and started stabbing her. Marr insisted that he did not sexually assault the victim. It is difficult to believe him on that score.

Convicted of second-degree murder, Edmond Jay Marr was sentenced to 16 years to life for the murder of Elaine Graham. He was sent on his way with the words of his victim's daughter resounding in his ears. "You've given me a life sentence of a broken heart," Elyse Graham told her mother's killer. "You've taken from me the most important person in the world."

Young Blood

Carol Hutto was 16 years old, and she had a major crush on a boy from her neighborhood, James Kuenn. The pair were juniors at Largo High School and, if classroom gossip was to be believed, they were dating. If those rumors were true, then Carol and James were keeping it a secret. Neither had admitted a relationship, not to their friends and not to their families.

On the evening of December 13, 1976, the phone started ringing at the Hutto residence in Largo, Florida. Carol ran to answer it and soon announced to the household, "It's for me." She then spent several minutes whispering down the line. By the time she hung up, she appeared flushed and excited. A short while later, she told her mother that she was taking a walk to the store. She was out of the door before anyone could ask questions.

Carol had told her mom that she would "not be long." That, of course, is an ambivalent statement, especially coming from a teenager. The walk to the store and back should have taken no more than twenty minutes. When Carol was still not back in an hour, her mother figured that she'd met one of her friends along the way and had stopped to talk. When two hours passed with no sight of her daughter, Norma Hutto began to become concerned. Eventually, she sent Carol's brother to look for her. He returned saying he couldn't find her.

By the following morning, everyone in the Hutto household was beside themselves with worry. Carol had still not returned and the police had been called in. But the family wasn't going to wait for them to begin their search. They fanned out across the neighborhood, knocking on doors, checking with Carol's friends, calling her name.

It was the missing girl's brother who had the misfortune of finding her. Carol Hutto was found submerged just below the surface of a neighborhood pond. But this was no accidental drowning. Someone had weighed down the teenager's body with a concrete block. An autopsy would later reveal that she had been strangled and struck on the head with some heavy object. Neither of those methods had killed her, though. Carol had still been alive when her killer tossed her into the pond. Water in her lungs proved that she had drowned.

But who would have done such an incredibly evil thing to an innocent girl, a girl with dreams of attending college, a girl whose whole life lay ahead of her? Carol's half-brother, Jerry Irwin, was briefly considered a suspect. Irwin was well known to police as a juvenile delinquent, and his whereabouts that night were unaccounted for. However, the focus of the investigation soon shifted to another teenager – 17-year-old James Kuenn.

There were plenty of reasons why Kuenn made a good suspect – his secret romance with the victim; entries in Carol's diary expressing her attraction to him; the phone call that Carol had received just before leaving the house. That had come from James, although he insisted that it had only been to discuss homework. He also denied meeting up with Carol that night. According to him, he'd never left his house. This wasn't exactly a watertight alibi, but it was difficult to disprove, and James Kuenn was sticking to it. He was one of the mourners at Carol's funeral where he expressed his heartfelt sympathies to her parents. He seemed as cut-up about Carol's death as any of her friends.

Over the next 18 months, the police worked the meager leads that they had but kept coming up against a brick wall. No one had seen Carol that night. She certainly hadn't made it to the store. The theory was that someone must have accosted her along the route, dragged her to some isolated spot and attacked her there. The location of that crime scene was unknown, and so too was the motive. Carol hadn't been robbed and she hadn't been raped. The police did have several hairs retrieved from the victim's body, but in those pre-DNA days, the evidence was of little use. Despite the best efforts of detectives, the case went cold.

While the investigation continued to flounder, while Carol's family continued to mourn their loss and pray for justice, James Kuenn was getting on with his life. After graduating high school, he joined the US Navy. He would enjoy a long and successful career in the military, rising to the rank of petty officer and serving as a submariner. By 1994, he had sixteen years of service behind him and was stationed at the U.S. Naval Submarine Base in Groton, Connecticut.

1994 was also the year that the Largo Police Department decided to take another pass at the Hutto case. The gist of this new probe was the hairs that had been found on Carol Hutto's body. These were submitted to the FBI lab, and a DNA profile was extracted. It did not find a match in any law enforcement database, but the investigators were not surprised by that. The suspect they had in mind did not have so much as a traffic violation against his name. Naval Petty Officer James Kuenn had lived an exemplary life.

What the police really needed was a biological sample for comparison against their profile. To this extent, they applied for a search warrant to draw blood from Kuenn. Since Kuenn was active duty Navy at that time, detectives also informed the Naval Criminal Investigative Services (NCIS) of their ongoing investigation. On July 15, 1998, a couple of the NCIS investigators brought Kuenn into an interrogation room and basically leaned on him. They told him that the Largo police had physical evidence linking him to a 1976 murder and recommended that he come clean while there were still options on the table.

It was a bluff, of course. The police had not yet made a DNA match. Nonetheless, Kuenn soon cracked. He admitted that he'd killed Carol Hutto but insisted that her death had been an accident. According to Kuenn, he and Carol had met up that night at a house under construction on Imperial Avenue, close to both of their homes. They had talked for a while, then started kissing and eventually had sex. After that, they started "kidding around," with Carol running through the house and Kuenn chasing her. But Carol had fallen during the chase and hit her head, rendering her unconscious. Kuenn said that he panicked at that point. He thought that Carol was dead and that he would be held responsible. He therefore decided to hide the body. Carrying Carol to a nearby pond, he threw her in and watched her sink below the surface. Then he walked home.

The problem with Kuenn's story was that it did not match the evidence. Carol's injuries were not consistent with a fall. She had been strangled and struck on the head. Still, Kuenn was sticking to his version of events. He would maintain this stance right until the eve of the trial when he decided to offer a new story. In this amended telling, Kuenn admitted that he and Carol had not had sex. He had wanted to, but she had resisted him. Then, as he persisted, things got physical. Carol started screaming, then scratching and hitting him. In response, he grabbed her by the throat and started squeezing. When he eventually released his grip, Carol collapsed to the floor.

From here, Kuenn's latest story picked up the narrative of his original telling. He'd panicked, he said, and decided to hide the body. Asked why he'd struck her on the head, he said it was to make it look like "someone else had done it," should her body be found. Nonetheless, the outcome for poor Carol was the same. She was brought to the pond and thrown in, weighed down by a concrete block. Kuenn swore that he'd had no idea she was still alive when she entered the water.

Of the two stories that Kuenn told, this one seems by far the more likely. Certainly, it tallies more closely with the evidence. Still, Kuenn's lawyers did not believe that his actions amounted to the first-degree charge the state had brought. At worst, it was third-degree murder, they argued, possibly even manslaughter.

Unfortunately for the defense, the jury did not agree. After just twenty-two minutes of deliberation, it returned its verdict – guilty of murder in the first degree. James Kuenn was sentenced to life in prison and must serve at least twenty-five years before he is eligible for parole. That will put him well into his 60s before he has a chance at freedom. But at least he has that chance. And at least he had a life before his misdeeds finally caught up with him. Carol Hutto had a mere 16 years before hers was cruelly snatched away.

Hollywood Ending

At 5:15 on the afternoon of January 6, 2001, Pam Shelly walked into the bathroom at the rural property she shared with her boyfriend in DeWitt County, Texas, placed a .32-caliber pistol to her temple and pulled the trigger. The bullet didn't kill her instantly. She was still alive when an EMS team arrived from Yorktown, some 20 miles away. Valuable time had already been lost by then and so the paramedics immediately loaded Pam into the ambulance. The nearest hospital was at Cuero. They needed to get her there as quickly as possible. That was when Pam's boyfriend, Ronnie Joe Hendrick, stepped in. He knew the quickest route he said and would direct them. He then scrambled into the cab. The ambulance was just racing away when the police arrived.

Pam Shelley's suicide attempt had been called in by her boyfriend's stepfather. And the Hendrick clan – Ronnie's mother, stepfather, and two brothers – were all eager to fill in the responding officers on the background to the tragedy. It appeared that Pam had been about to leave Texas, where she'd lived the previous five months, to return to her native Arkansas. She had been none too keen on making the trip but had been forced into it because her 12-year-old daughter, Kayla, was finding it difficult to settle. The child, apparently, had behavioral issues and caused her mother no end of problems. It all meant that Pam would have to end her relationship with Ronnie and that deeply distressed her. Aggravating the issue was her ongoing battle with depression and a history of suicide that ran through her family.

The way that this testimony had been presented seemed to support the initial notion of a self-inflicted gunshot wound. And the theory was backed up by evidence found inside the house. In the bathroom, deputies located a 32-caliber revolver and a holster. They also found a spent bullet, blood-spatter on the tile, and a small puddle of blood on the floor. While all of this was ongoing, Pam Shelly had made it alive to the emergency room at Cuero. From there, she was airlifted to a specialist gunshot unit in San Antonio. Unfortunately, the desperate effort to save her life would not succeed. She died that night.

Ronnie Hendrick was questioned by the police, of course, and told much the same story as his parents and siblings. Pam had been depressed about ending their relationship and returning to Arkansas. He'd been standing outside the house when he'd heard the gunshot. He'd sprinted inside and had found her lying, gravely injured, on the bathroom floor. Desperate, he'd phoned his stepfather, asking what to do. His stepfather had then called 911.

There was one major inconsistency in Ronnie Hendrick's story, one that the police did not pick up at the time. According to Ronnie, Pam was only returning to Arkansas because she feared losing her children – Kayla and her younger brother, Dustin – if she remained in Texas. But if that was the case, if she was desperate not to be separated from her kids, why would she then kill herself and lose them forever? It didn't make sense.

Perhaps the reason that investigators did not pursue this issue was because the autopsy report seemed to back up Ronnie's story. The gunshot was a contact wound to the right temple. The trajectory of the bullet was front to back, down to up and right to left. It was, in other words, a classic suicide wound. Factor in witness testimony as to the victim's state of mind, and it is easy to see why the medical examiner ruled the death a suicide.

But not everyone was happy with this outcome. Senior investigators at the DeWitt County Sherriff's Department wanted another crack at Ronnie Hendrick and asked him to take a polygraph. Ronnie initially agreed but skipped out on the first two appointments and then skipped out altogether. When officers went to follow up with him, they found that he'd left the area. His parents and siblings professed to have no knowledge of his whereabouts.

And so the case languished, confined to a dusty file at the back of a cabinet, not even a cold case really, since Pam's death was officially a suicide. It would remain so for the next seven years, until Jody Zavesky was voted in as DeWitt County Sheriff. Zavesky had barely taken office when he was approached by a detective named Carl Bowen, a veteran of the DeWitt County force. Bowen had never bought Ronnie Hendrick's story about how Pam Shelly had died and had always been suspicious of his disappearance just when he was due to take a polygraph. He wanted to reopen the investigation. In spite of a heavy workload of active cases, the Sherriff agreed that he could

That would turn out to be a well-timed decision. Ronnie Hendrick had been off the radar for seven years but in the summer of 2008, he showed up again in DeWitt County. And not just in the county but in the county jail, after he was arrested for beating up his current girlfriend. Looking into Hendrick's activities during his self-imposed exile, Bowen learned that he'd been living in South Dakota, where he'd spent time locked up on a felony DUI.

Bowen's next move was to visit Hendrick at the County lockup and ask him to make good on the agreement he'd made all those years earlier and take a polygraph. Hendrick could easily have refused. However, he was probably aware of how that would look. Refusal, coupled with his earlier evasiveness, would make him appear guilty.

And so Hendrick agreed to take the polygraph…and failed. When Bowen then tried to ask some follow up questions, he refused and asked for a lawyer. Bowen did learn, however, that Hendrick had been talking to his fellow inmates. According to the story he was peddling, he'd been present when Pam Shelly shot herself. This wasn't an admission to wrongdoing but it was a different story to the one he'd told the police. And if he'd lied about that, what else was he lying about?

As it turned out, Hendrick (and his family) had been lying about quite a lot. Pam hadn't suffered from depression and there was no history of suicide in her family. Her reason for returning to Arkansas was also not what they said it was. She wasn't leaving Texas to placate her daughter. She was doing it to escape the frequent beatings handed out by Ronnie Joe Hendrick.

It was a far from conclusive case. Yet Bowen felt that there was enough circumstantial evidence to disprove suicide. And if Pam hadn't killed herself then the only other option was murder, of which there was only one suspect. Armed with this, Bowen took his case to the District Attorney. He probably knew that he was reaching and could not have been entirely surprised when he was turned down. It wasn't that the D.A. did not believe in Hendrick's guilt. It was just not a winnable case.

Over the next four years, the Shelly investigation went nowhere, stalled for lack of conclusive evidence. Then, in 2012, Hollywood came to town. Carl Bowen was approached by a true crime show called Cold Justice, which wanted to profile the Pam Shelly case. The show had a unique concept, investigating real cold cases in conjunction with jurisdictions which would otherwise not have the resources to pursue them, offering investigative support and access to the latest forensic technologies. With former Harris County ADA Kelly Siegler involved, plus a former crime scene investigator in Yolanda McClary, this was potentially a godsend to understaffed and under-budgeted law enforcement agencies. When Bowen approached the D.A. for permission to proceed, he received a cautious approval.

The results, though, were disappointing. DNA tests on the gun turned up a match to the victim and no one else. Ditto Pam's bloodstained t-shirt. Ballistics confirmed that the bullet was from the .32 but the police already knew that. Background checks confirmed what Bowen had already uncovered – that the Hendrick clan had lied about Pam's state of mind, her supposed use of anti-depressants and her reasons for leaving Texas. There was also confirmation of Ronnie Hendrick's violent tendencies, his attacks on numerous female partners, both before and after Pam's death. None of it amounted to evidence of murder.

In the end, it was the work of Carl Bowen, not the Cold Justice team, that persuaded the D.A. to bring the case to trial. Bowen had tracked Pam's ex-husband, Jessie, to a Texas prison where he was serving time. According to Jessie, he and Pam had been planning to get back together before she was killed. In fact, he'd spoken to her on the day she died. During the course of that conversation, Hendrick had ripped the phone away and shouted down the line that the only way Pam was coming back to Arkansas was in a pine box. This was a direct threat, uttered by the chief suspect just hours before the victim was shot to death. It was, though, based on the word of a convicted felon and thus of questionable value. Jessie was asked to repeat his allegations while hooked up to a polygraph. He immediately agreed and passed with flying colors. It was then that the D.A. agreed to bring the case before a grand jury.

Ronnie Joe Hendrick was indicted for murder in November 2012, with his trial set for September 2013. In the meantime, he remained in jail on the assault charge. But this already convoluted case was about to take another twist. The pilot episode of "Cold Justice" was due to air on September 3, with the producers determined that it would feature the Shelley case. Despite submissions from the D.A. asking them to delay the broadcast, they remained determined to go ahead.

The result was inevitable. When the matter came before the court, it proved impossible to find a juror who had not watched the broadcast and formed an opinion on the case. When the judge polled potential jurors for their opinion, eleven of the twelve admitted that they believed Ronnie Hendrick had killed Pam Shelly. That left no option but to declare a mistrial. A new date was set for June 2014. The defense immediately filed for a change of venue.

The premise behind "Cold Justice" is that it provides support to small law enforcement agencies in solving cold cases while at the same time documenting the process for prime time viewing. The police get an unsolved case off their books; the TV station gets a compelling real life drama; the victim's loved ones get much-delayed justice. Everybody wins except for the perpetrator, who is finally made to pay for his crimes. In this case, however, the show had not delivered on its part of the bargain. It could even be said that it had hindered the prosecution.

But Cold Justice was about to pay its dues in an unexpected way. With the trial delayed, the D.A. decided to make an approach to the defense, citing the impact of the program. The evidence presented therein was the same evidence that he would rely on in court. Clearly, the jurors had found it convincing. Did the defense really believe that another jury would come to a different conclusion? Hendrick was going down, looking at life without parole. His only hope was to negotiate a plea deal.

In the end, Ronnie Hendrick must have seen the hopelessness of his situation. This brutish man, who routinely used the women in his life as punching bags, had been backed into a corner. With nowhere to turn, he decided to accept the offer the D.A. was dangling in front of him, 22 years in prison in exchange for his guilty plea. Only now would the truth be known. How he'd snuck up on Pam, pressed the gun to her temple and warned her not to move; how he'd pulled the trigger and then lowered her limp body to the floor; how he'd left her lying in a pool of her own blood for over an hour before asking his stepfather to call 911; how he and his family had used that hour to get their stories straight.

And it had almost worked. But for the persistence of a dedicated detective and the roundabout help of a TV crew, Ronnie Hendrick would have gotten away with murder. Now, he was going to pay for what he'd done. Cold Justice had its Hollywood ending.

For more True Crime books by Robert Keller

please visit:
http://bit.ly/kellerbooks

Printed in Great Britain
by Amazon

24098363R00076